FAILURE

AND

PROGRESS

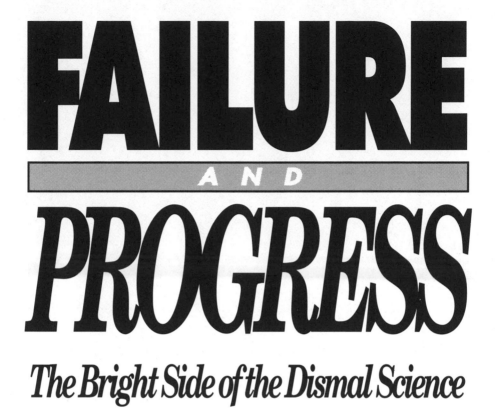

FAILURE

AND

PROGRESS

The Bright Side of the Dismal Science

Dwight R. Lee and Richard B. McKenzie

CATO
INSTITUTE
Washington D.C.

Library of Congress Cataloging-in-Publication Data

Lee, Dwight R.
    Failure and progress : the bright side of the dismal science /
Dwight R. Lee and Richard B. McKenzie.
      p.   cm.
    Includes bibliographical references and index.
    ISBN 1-882577-03-5 : $19.95.—ISBN 1-882577-02-7 : $10.95 (pbk.)
    1. Economic policy. 2. Economic security. I. McKenzie, Richard
B. II. Title.
HD87.L44   1993   93-16921
338.9—dc20   CIP

Cover Design by Colin Moore.

Printed in the United States of America.

Cato Institute
224 Second Street, S.E.
Washington, D.C. 20003

To Betty Tillman

Contents

Preface

By any measure of economic success, socialism has been a total failure. The hope of socialism was that it would promote wealth and distribute it fairly by transferring power away from capitalists interested only in profits and giving more control to political representatives concerned with economic growth and social justice. That hope has been dashed. Socialism has succeeded only in providing special privileges to a few by imposing grinding poverty on everyone else.

With socialism a sinking ship, the goal in country after country that has been impoverished by the legacy of Karl Marx is to achieve the wealth-creating power of capitalism. The most dramatic examples of the rejection of socialism and the move to embrace capitalism have come from countries of Eastern Europe and the Soviet Union itself—countries that have experienced the poverty of socialism firsthand. But countries in Africa, South America, and other parts of the world that had been beguiled by the false promises of socialism also are anxious to trade socialism for capitalism.

Although the embrace of the market economy has been widespread, it has also been cautious. Many people want the wealth created by capitalism, but they also perceive the marketplace as being harsh, callous, and unfair. Isn't the market place littered with the victims of those who have suffered the failure of bankruptcy, unemployment, and poverty at the unmerciful hands of market competition? Isn't there some way to accept the wealth that capitalism offers without having to endure the constant failures it imposes? The calls have been for a market economy with a human face or for a third way between the productivity of capitalism and the compassion of socialism. And there is no end to politically inspired proposals to reform the marketplace to protect its innocent victims.

However, contrary to the wishes of persistent critics, capitalism is a bundle of coherent and inextricable attributes. Of course, it would be nice to unbundle the economic package known as capitalism, or the free market, and keep the sweet while rejecting the bitter. It would also be nice if everyone had an above-average income. Unfortunately, the only way to avoid the failures that result from capitalism is to pass up the wealth that results from capitalism. Failures in the marketplace serve an indispensable function in the production of wealth; they provide both information on the most productive use of resources and the motivation for people to respond appropriately to that information. Failures are part of the steering mechanism that directs an economy toward prosperity. Attempting to improve the marketplace by preventing economic failure is equivalent to attempting to improve an automobile by removing the steering wheel. It is no surprise that socialist economies that were applauded initially for eliminating unemployment, bankruptcies, and economic failure of every variety have themselves been colossal economic failures. By allowing economic failures in the small, and converting these failures into useful information, market economies have produced economic success in the large. In economics, overall success depends on a constant supply of small failures.

As economists, we favor the market as the best means for organizing most economic activity. Thus, we believe it is important that the role of economic failure be understood as necessary to the advantages derived from the marketplace. Conveying that message is our overriding objective in this book. There are six important points that are developed and that can be briefly covered here.

First, although economic failure is a positive force in a market economy, it has to be recognized that there is no economy, market or otherwise, that stands apart from the political process. Every economy is a political economy, and for the very reason that economic failure promotes wealth in the marketplace, it also promotes political responses that can undermine the market process. A public understanding of the importance of economic failure is the best way to moderate harmful political responses to that failure. The lack of understanding of the essential role of economic failure stands as the biggest political obstacle to achieving free-market prosperity in formerly socialist countries. The same lack of understanding also prevents the market process from yielding the full measure of its potential wealth in those political economies that are predominantly capitalist.

Second, it is easy to see the failures imposed by the market as isolated occurrences rather than as an integral part of a wealth-creating process. When economic failure is viewed in isolation, it is natural to see it as unnecessarily harsh and unfair and to conclude that government can protect people against such failure without harming economic productivity. And if government can, at little cost, protect people against failures unfairly imposed upon them by market forces, then surely social justice must require that it do so. But government cannot protect everyone against failure. The best government can do is to protect a privileged few against failure by diminishing the opportunity for success of everyone else. Obviously, such special-interest protection is neither efficient nor fair.

Third, and ironically, for the very reasons that it is both more efficient and fair than alternative economic systems, the market economy appears to be unfair to the superficial observer. The efficiency of the market process derives from the fact that it holds people accountable for the costs of their actions. Those costs are concentrated on market participants in ways that are difficult for them to ignore, and they are commonly imposed through the harshness of bankruptcy, unemployment, and other forms of economic failure. Although this market accountability conveys long-run benefits on all by promoting productivity, each economic interest group prefers to be protected against the accountability of the market while benefiting from the accountability the market is imposing on others. In the marketplace, such free riding on the contribution of others is not allowed, and that is the basis for the fundamental fairness of the market. In the marketplace, all people have to contribute to the general well-being by accepting the failures as well as the successes that come their way. However, because the benefits from market accountability are general, they are easily ignored and taken for granted. Because the costs and failures of market accountability are concentrated, they easily dominate the public's perception of the market and create the impression of unfairness. Indeed, the failures inflicted by the market appear all the more unfair against the backdrop of the economic success made possible by those failures.

Fourth, for the very reasons that the political process is typically less efficient and fair than the market process, it appears to be fair to the superficial observer. A major source of the inefficiency resulting from the political process derives from the fact that it provides opportunities for people to acquire benefits without being held accountable for the full costs. Political action commonly concentrates benefits on a well-organized few while spreading the costs thinly over the general public. As opposed to the fairness of the market process, the political process encourages some to free ride on the contributions of others. Because political benefits are concentrated, however, they are easily noticed, greatly appreciated, and readily associated with particular policies and politicians. Because the costs are spread over so many, they are easily ignored. The impression conveyed is that the political process prompts generosity and mitigates the unfairness of the marketplace. And the larger the number of people receiving political benefits and the poorer the market operates because of the increasing burden of government, the more fairness seems to demand extending political benefits to yet additional recipients.

Fifth, the impression that failure in the marketplace is unfair and government action to moderate that failure is fair is accentuated by special-interest politics. No matter how well a group is organized politically, it is not likely to be successful in obtaining special-interest subsidies, protections, and other exemptions from the discipline of market competition if it tries to argue that its members want to benefit at the expense of the general public. A far more effective argument for a special interest is that both it and the public interest are being threatened with bankruptcy, job losses, and dislocations by unfair market forces. Whether it is farmers facing foreclosure, steelworkers facing indefinite layoffs, or Chrysler Corporation facing bankruptcy, the group's chances of appealing to public compassion and obtaining political protections against market pressures are increased with a persuasive argument that those pressures are unfair.

Sixth, with public compassion being exploited by interest groups using economic failure as a pretense for capturing special privileges, the result is unlikely to be very compassionate. There are certainly people who, for reasons beyond their control, are left behind in the marketplace and who deserve sympathy and help. Unfortunately, those who need help the most are the ones whom political action in the name of compassion helps the least. Pointing to the problem of poverty has long been the most effective way of disparaging the market economy and persuading the public that, in the absence of government programs, the marketplace would be littered with the poor and the desperate. What has been almost completely ignored is the government's impotence in helping the poor. Indeed, various studies suggest strongly that, by reducing the productivity of the marketplace, government transfer programs have reduced the income of the poor. By concentrating attention on the economic failures in the marketplace to justify expanding political control over economic decisions, the influence of special-interest demands has been increased and the scope of economic failure has been enlarged.

This book was written with the conviction that unless economic failure is understood as integral to the successful performance of market economies, it will be seized upon by active political interests as justification for expanding government action that stifles general economic productivity for the short-run advantage of the politically influential few. As long as the economic failures that impose the guiding discipline in market economies are widely perceived as unnecessary and unfair, a threat remains to the prosperity of existing capitalist economies, and a roadblock stands in the path of economic progress in those economies that are trying to escape the blight of socialism.

Although our book is short, the list of people and institutions that assisted us in the writing of it is long. Our colleagues George Selgin, Richard Timberlake, and Larry White have read parts of the manuscript at various stages and have made useful comments. The Liberty Fund sponsored a conference around a long paper that served as the nucleus of the book. The written comments of Paul Heyne, William Mitchell, and Kenneth MacKenzie presented at the conference, as well as the general discussion, were responsible for numerous improvements in both the content and exposition of the final product. Thanks are also due to the Center for the Study of American Business at Washington University, where both authors were John M. Olin visiting scholars for a year (McKenzie during the 1985–86 academic year and Lee during the 1988–89 academic year) and where significant portions of the early writing on this book were done. Murray Weidenbaum and Kenneth Chilton provided many useful comments and editorial suggestions during this period. Kristin Johnson deserves special appreciation for her patience and skill in typing and retyping the manuscript, and for her insightful responses from the perspective of a noneconomist.

Dwight Lee would like to thank the Philip M. McKenna Foundation for the general financial assistance it has provided his work over the last few years. Richard McKenzie must thank the John M. Olin Foundation and the Lynde and Harry Bradley Foundation for supporting his work at times during the period this book was developed. Special thanks must go to the Earhart Foundation, which provided us with a joint summer research grant to put our earlier writing and thoughts into book form.

And finally, though she had no direct involvement with the writing of this book, we want to thank Betty Tillman of the Center for Study of Public Choice at George Mason University for her wonderful presence in our academic lives. We both spent important years at the Center for Study of Public Choice at Virginia Tech and George Mason. These years were more productive and pleasant because of Betty's competence, cheerfulness, and charm. We dedicate this book to her.

1. In Consideration of Failure

There is an old saying that success has many parents, but failure is always born an orphan. No one wants to experience failure or to be held responsible for it. Individuals go to great lengths to avoid failure, and when they are unsuccessful, as is persistently the case, they are easily convinced that the causes lie beyond their control.

Yet it is also recognized that the economic success of individuals, as well as the success of the general economy, depends upon failure. The person who is successful is typically one who has attempted difficult tasks and who has failed at many—often most—of them. Each failure provides information that the successful person pays attention to and uses in future endeavors. A critical feature of—and major reason for—the success of decentralized market economies is that such economies send clear signals of failure in the form of depressed profits and prices to those who are making poor use of their resources. People either respond appropriately to these signals or experience personal economic failure in the form of losses that transfer their resources to others who will make more productive use of them.

Although people do recognize the importance of failure, typically they do so grudgingly. Their dominant reaction to failure is quite naturally a negative one. That is as it should be, given that it is people's intense aversion to failure, along with their equally intense desire for success, that motivate appropriate market responses to the information provided by prices and profits. But economic failure can motivate more than market responses. Individuals and organized groups often find advantage in taking political action in attempts to avoid the threat and consequences of economic failure. Their attempts are often facilitated by public opinion that sympathizes with those who have suffered financial hardship and that sees economic failure as a social problem requiring corrective action.

Not only do victims of economic failure see advantage in government efforts to assist them, but large numbers of public employees

1

have an interest in government programs that attempt to address problems of economic failure. Few academic researchers or government commissions study failure, except to lament its consequences and to formulate what they believe to be corrective solutions. The strong tendency is for the political process to concentrate on the negative side of failure and ignore the positive contributions to our economic well-being that flow from failure. This tendency is pernicious because it commonly leads to government activity that increases the general failure in the economy through inept attempts to reduce specific failures in the economy.

Because we, like others, are not fond of failure, we believe it is important to focus on the bright side of failures, especially the economic failures experienced in the marketplace. Our purpose here is not to simply lament the harm caused by failure but to study the conditions under which the failure that is inevitable can generate the most benefit. Economic failure is an understudied and underappreciated side of economic progress. By helping to develop a more informed and tolerant public opinion on failure, we hope to counter the public pressure that causes government to respond to failure with public policies that retard economic progress and promote greater failure. Indeed, our central thesis can be stated succinctly: failure is the nursemaid of progress, and vice versa.

Nevertheless, we fully recognize the emotional reaction to failures and the desire of well-meaning people to do something about them. In this book, we explore the reasons that political leaders so frequently devise agendas to rectify apparent cases of failure. However, we concentrate on the potential harm resulting from collective efforts to mitigate economic failure by blunting corrective responses to that failure. Direct public solutions to failure—those that often seem most obvious—are invariably less effective than advertised, and they commonly aggravate the very problem they are suppose to solve.

Our purpose is to unravel the essential insight that the late Joseph Schumpeter, professor of political economy at Harvard University, summarized as "creative destruction." Schumpeter's fundamental insight was to recognize that "A system—any system, economic or other—that at *every* given point of time fully utilizes its possibilities to the best advantage may yet in the long run be inferior to a system that does so at *no* point of time, because the latter's failure to do so may be a condition for the level or speed of long-run performance."[1] The wisdom contained in this short passage can be appreciated only when there is an understanding of the linkages that exist within the marketplace between failure and success. Those linkages are the focus of much of the following discussion. But first it is useful to have a brief statistical perspective on economic failure and success in the United States.

The Abundance of Success and Failure

The economic history of any country is typically written with considerable attention being given to the successes of its people. Accordingly, the economic history of the United States is generally viewed with much reverence for the growth in the country's well-being, which typically is evaluated in terms of the rise in gross national product (GNP), industrial assets and productivity, consumer purchases, jobs, and personal income.

Figure 1.1 shows four decades of success in national production as measured by GNP in terms of constant (1982) dollars. Between 1947 and 1990, real GNP almost quintupled, from just over $1 trillion to nearly $5 trillion. Of course, because the country's population rose during the period, real per capita GNP rose more modestly, but still more than doubled. (See Figure 1.2.)

During the 1947–90 period, industrial production escalated more than fivefold, and the output of manufactured goods expanded even more. (See Figure 1.3.) Granted, the growth in production required slightly more than twice the number of workers, but, on average, each person worked significantly fewer hours a week. The substantial growth in worker productivity during the period explains why total output expanded by several times more than the increase in the labor force.

Nevertheless, none of these measures of economic success fully accounts for the substantial improvement during this century in the quality of the goods and services produced, in the nature of work and play, or in the control that many people have over their lives. Cars start on cold mornings with much greater ease than they did in the 1930s. Many foods bought in grocery stores are

---

[1]Joseph A. Schumpeter, *Capitalism, Socialism, and Democracy* , 2nd ed. (New York: Harper & Brothers Publishers, 1947), p. 83 (emphasis in original).

Figure 1.1
GROSS NATIONAL PRODUCT, 1947–1990
(IN 1982 DOLLARS)

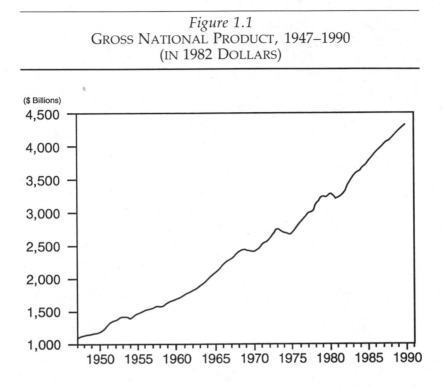

SOURCE: *Economic Report of the President* (Washington: Government Printing Office, 1991).

safer and more conveniently packaged for ready use. People no longer need to live close to work, or, because of new modes of communications, they don't even have to leave their homes to go to work. In short, the quality of the goods and services produced during the last 60 years probably has grown by far more than the actual volume of output.

Americans cherish the thought that no other people on earth can produce as much, spend as much, travel as much, or play as much as they can. They are proud of the fact that people from other countries praise them for their inventiveness, or "Yankee ingenuity." They boast of how many people from other countries around the world want to move to the United States in order to benefit from the American system that produces so much success. Americans

Figure 1.2
GROSS NATIONAL PRODUCT PER CAPITA, 1947–1990
(IN 1982 DOLLARS)

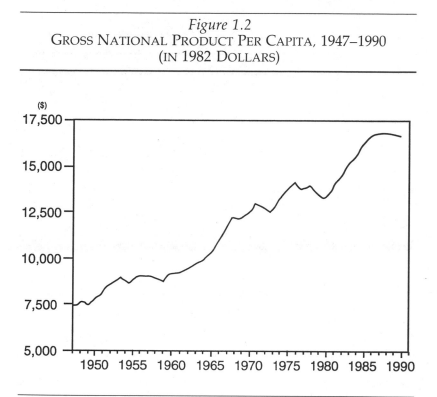

SOURCE: *Economic Report of the President* (Washington: Government Printing Office, 1991).

recognize that immigration is proof that the United States must be doing something right, especially when people in other countries are willing to risk life and limb to experience the opportunities that Americans take for granted.

Americans love to tout the prices of their cars and boats and to count the number of educated youth, fast-food restaurants, personal computers, and lanes on expressways—all measures of success. They go into mourning when their national athletic teams win fewer medals at international games than teams from other countries. They want always to succeed and never to fail, or so it seems.

The economic successes of the country abound, and the measures of successes are almost as varied as the people. Americans are

5

Figure 1.3
INDUSTRIAL PRODUCTION INDEX, 1947–1991 (1987 = 100)

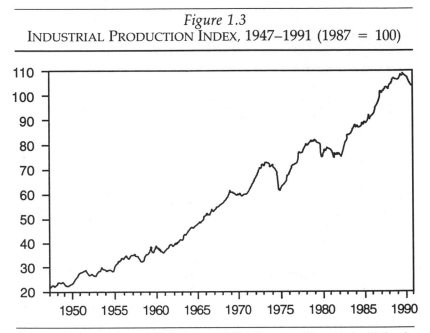

SOURCE: Citibank Economic Database, 1946–Present (New York, Citibank, N.A., 1978). The database is a machine-readable magnetic data file.

understandably pleased with what they have accomplished in a relatively short span of history since the country was founded as an independent nation. Success has been the hallmark of the U.S. economy. Indeed, in terms of living standards, few people in the history of mankind have been more successful. Americans are a truly fortunate people.

Nonetheless, the economic history of the country is also a saga of failures—of lost jobs, income, and wealth. It is a story of hardship and problems—lots of problems—portrayed vividly by recurring episodes of recession, stagnation, stagflation, and unemployment, and by the persistence of poverty.

In no small way, failures are endemic to the U.S. economy. In 1989, 643,000 business and nonbusiness bankruptcy petitions were filed, nearly 11 times the number in 1929; that same year, 1989, was marked by the failure of 50,400 commercial and industrial businesses with total uncovered liabilities in excess of $44 billion.[2]

[2]See Bureau of the Census, *Statistical Abstract of the United States: 1991* (Washington: Government Printing Office, 1991), Table 881.

Furthermore, the failure rate in the late 1980s was much higher than it had been several decades earlier. In 1989 the business-failure rate broached 65, meaning that 65 of every 10,000 "listed" businesses failed, whereas in 1945 the rate had been only 4.[3]

Failure, not success, is the fate of most small businesses. To the casual observer, that point is evidenced by the number of empty storefronts in the downtown areas of any sizable city. Most small businesses start on a shoestring and end up with little more than memories of how the business was held together as long as possible. Many fold the first year; almost all are closed within five years. Only the exceptional enterprises expand beyond the small-business category.

Very large corporations are often thought to be indestructible, perhaps more durable than governments, but even those businesses have a difficult time surviving for more than a few decades. Just ask someone under 30, "What is a Packard?" or even, "What was People Express?"

Even over short periods of time, the Fortune 500, the country's 500 largest publicly held corporations, is in constant flux. In 1986, for example, almost 10 percent of the companies that had been on the list in 1985 left the Fortune 500 as they were taken over by other companies or lost sales and market share; 70 of the 500 lost money, with one listed company, LTV, managing to lose $3.25 billion, the largest annual net loss ever endured by an American corporation.[4] Having failed miserably, LTV filed for bankruptcy, to no one's surprise. In 1991, Pan American Airlines, once the proud master of the international skies, was selling off its components as rapidly as the bankruptcy court would allow. Pan Am was not alone in its failure. Over 200 American airlines failed in the late 1980s.

Even when companies do not fail, many of their processes and products go out of existence and many of their plants are closed (as new processes and plants are started). In 1983 and 1984, the U.S. General Accounting Office (GAO) found that 25 percent of the country's firms having 50 or more workers closed at least one

---

[3]Ibid., Table 884.

[4]Stephen J. Madden and Julianne Slovak, "A Year of Pain and Promise," *Fortune* (April 27, 1987), pp. 360–61. IBM has since broken that unenviable record.

plant.[5] That means that during the two-year period covered by the GAO survey, more than 16,000 plants with 50 or more workers were closed and 1.3 million workers were affected.[6]

The layoff rate from closed plants slowed down in the late 1980s, but only moderately, remaining at over a million workers a year. The manufacturing sector accounted for 60 percent of the closed plants having 100 or more workers. Slightly more than 13 percent of the nation's estimated 35,000 manufacturing plants with 100 or more workers were closed.[7] The closure rate for large manufacturing plants varied by region, from under 7 percent in the east south central region to over 19 percent in the New England and west south central regions.[8] Yet products continue to proliferate.

Unemployment, which assesses the ability of people to find and retain jobs, is probably the most widely cited measure of failure. The GAO found that in the 1981–86 period, more than 13 million workers lost their jobs and 90 percent of those workers were "permanently displaced," meaning their layoffs were not seasonal or temporary.[9] Of the permanently displaced workers, 85 percent, or more than nine million, had more than one year of job tenure, and more than five million had more than five years of job tenure.[10] Many of these workers not only lost their incomes; they lost their careers when their firms failed. Some of the unemployed had to take to the streets to find a living, and some ended up living in the streets (or in parks or abandoned buildings). Homelessness is a product of devastating and often persistent economic and human failure.[11]

[5]William J. Gainer, *Dislocated Workers: Extent of Closures, Layoffs, and the Public and Private Response*, GAO/HDR-86-116BR (Washington: Government Printing Office, July 1986), pp. 1, 2.

[6]An additional 2.3 million workers in plants with fewer than 50 workers also lost their jobs to plant closures and permanent layoffs. Ibid., pp. 10–11.

[7]Ibid., p. 11.

[8]Ibid., p. 14.

[9]Ibid.

[10]Ibid.

[11]It should also be recognized that the problem of homelessness is worsened by rent controls and a host of government regulations on land use and construction standards that are often the result of special-interest political influence and that always result in higher costs for housing. For a comprehensive study of this problem, see M. Bruce Johnson, ed., *Resolving the Housing Crisis: Government Policy, Decontrol, and the Public Interest* (San Francisco: Pacific Institute for Public Policy Research, 1982).

Poverty is the ultimate destination of those who consistently encounter economic failure. In 1990, 7 million families, or 33.4 million Americans, lived below the official poverty-income level.[12] Even though the poverty rate fell that year to below 14 percent from slightly above 15 percent in 1983, the incidence of poverty was still higher in 1990 than it had been throughout the 1970s.[13] Many of those in the poverty count were children whose continued failure in life was being made likely by the inability of their parents (mainly single mothers) to pay for proper prenatal care and to provide the family stability and support conducive to upward economic mobility. Without question, the much discussed cycle of poverty translates for many Americans into recurring cycles of failure.[14]

The poor, of course, are not the only ones who fail. In fact, most failures may be endured by the rich, because the rich have more to venture and more opportunities to lose what they have. The failure of the well-to-do has probably never been more apparent than it was on October 19, 1987, when the stock market fell by more than 500 points, wiping out at least one-half trillion dollars of investors' wealth.

The pervasiveness of failures is made clear in many nonstatistical ways. The continuous flow of news reports on this or that closed

[12]*Economic Report of the President* (Washington: Government Printing Office, 1991), p. 330.

[13]Ibid.

[14]There is no consensus on the origins of the cycle of poverty. Most commentators suggest that it emerges from cultural deprivation, a denial of resources that, if they were available, would enable poor people to lift themselves up by their bootstraps. However, an alternative explanation suggests that the cycle occurs because

> people experience a social isolation that excludes them from the job network system that permeates other neighborhoods and that is so important in learning about or being recommended for jobs that become available in various parts of the city. . . .
> Thus, in such neighborhoods the chances are overwhelming that children will seldom interact on a sustained basis with people who are employed or with families that have a steady breadwinner. . . . The development of cognitive, linguistic, and other educational and job-related skills necessary for the world of work in the mainstream economy is thereby adversely affected. . . . A vicious cycle is perpetuated through the family, through the community, and through the schools.

William Julius Wilson, *The Truly Disadvantaged: The Inner City, the Underclass, and Public Policy* (Chicago: University of Chicago Press, 1987), p. 57.

plant, this or that firm that has gone belly-up, or this or that group of workers that has had to face poverty speaks eloquently of the inadequacy of any set of statistics to capture either the prevalence or impact of economic failures in the lives of Americans. Given the attention bestowed by the media and politics on malfunctioning consumer products, collapsing banks and stock market prices, foreclosed farms, and expanding trade deficits, the casual reader of today's news may understandably think that Americans love to brood over their failures as much as they like to extol their successes.

The Direction of the Study

If one wants to understand the important social issues of the day, one has to understand the role of failure in shaping the U.S. economy. Failure is not only the output of unsuccessful economic activity; it is also an essential input of a successful economy.

Our purpose here is not to whitewash failure or to pretend that failure is an unmitigated social blessing. But because the overwhelming tendency is to emphasize the dark side of failure, we believe it is important to add balance to the discussion of social issues by focusing on the bright side of failure. Indeed, it is our view that productive public policy in response to failure is impossible as long as public opinion sees failure only in negative terms.

Our central theme is that economic activity is always a two-edged sword, a continuing chronicle of rampant success trimmed by the cutting edge of widespread failure. And it is no accident that we juxtapose statistical reviews of successes and failures. Throughout U.S. history, success and failure appear to have been inseparable, with each practically the mirror image of the other. Indeed, it is hard to see how progress could possibly be made without concurrent failures. That is true because progress implies improvement, and improvement implies replacement. A better mousetrap necessarily takes the place of an old mousetrap. The first ballpoint pens, introduced in the late 1940s, replaced many fountain pens and pencils. Large mechanical calculators and slide rules were replaced by the first hand-held calculators. Today, fax machines are beginning to replace the service provided by the door-to-door postman, file cabinets are being replaced by computer memory, phonograph records are being replaced by tapes and compact disks, etc.

Displacement necessarily means that something will fail, in the sense that plants will be shut down, workers will be unemployed, incomes will be lost, and lives will be disrupted, at least for a while. The only economy that could be free of failure is one that was completely stagnant and devoid of economic progress. Nothing would then have to change, and nothing would then have to be ventured or lost—except the opportunity for a better life.

On the surface, the subject of this monograph may appear to be a dismal one (fully fit for practitioners of the "dismal science" of economics), but we don't see our study in that light. On the contrary, because we see a positive side to failure, we see its instructive qualities, its productive consequences, and its inevitable association with success. As opposed to being dismal, the central concern of our monograph is the inextricable connection between economic success (and progress) and economic failure; it is concerned with how and why economic success and failure go hand in hand. Our purpose is to explore the ways in which economic success spawns economic failure, and vice versa, and to explain why it is reasonable to conclude that the more rapid the success, the more prevalent the failure.

The caveat that is in order here is that the benefits derived from failure are not independent of the economic institutions that are in place. We focus on economic failures within market economies for one principal reason: market economies tend to be the more dynamic, more progressive, and more successful economies because they make more productive use of failures by motivating the appropriate responses to them. Also, specific failures in market economies are often the unavoidable consequences of, and therefore necessary to, general economic success.

Our study of economic failure must, of course, carry us beyond the strict confines of economic science. We detect an inherent conflict between the needs of a market economy and the needs of democratic politics. The conflict emerges precisely because both systems thrive on economic failures, although for decidedly different reasons. As noted, market economies need failures to give direction to people's efforts to work, save, and invest—efficiently. Democratic politics, on the other hand, is often driven to mitigate failures, simply because in the context of individual political decisions, constrained and directed by the short time horizons of the election cycles, failures can easily be seen as unfair and unjust, if not downright cruel. Economic failures provide fuel for political struggles that, as discussed later in this book, may reduce the failure of a few in the short run at the expense of increasing the failure of many in the long run.

Concluding Comments

No one wants to fail, yet people might choose an economic system that not only allows failure but also highlights its harmful consequences. Failure in the national economy serves much the same purpose as pain in the human body. Although no one wants to endure pain, people are grateful to have bodies that register pain, because otherwise they would be highly vulnerable to major injury and early death. Just as pain and the threat of pain prompt action to avoid physical harm and promote physical well-being, failure and the threat of failure prompt action to avoid economic harm and promote economic well-being. Indeed, failure is a more positive feature of the economy than pain is of the body, in that pain is primarily a signal of physical problems and is seldom a direct consequence of physical vitality. For reasons that are elaborated on in the next chapter, failure not only serves to steer the economy into productive channels but also is a necessary and direct result of economic progress.

The benefits of failure do not and should not harden our hearts to those who suffer from economic hardships for reasons beyond their control. Most people feel some desire to assist those who are in unfortunate circumstances, and it is all too natural for individuals to want others to share, through the political process, the burden of their compassion and concern. Unfortunately, the political process is an extremely blunt instrument for dealing with particular cases of economic failure. Although political action can alleviate the burden of failure for some, it does so by redistributing the burden to others. Such a spreading of the burden of failure can be socially productive if it results from political action that is properly directed. But political action is seldom well focused on any one objective and, more often than not, political attempts to address particular cases of economic failure do little to reduce that failure but much to hamper success elsewhere in the economy.

Just as there are economic failures, so also there are political failures. And in the case of political failure, there is an absence of the type of feedback mechanism that exists in market economies to use failure as an informative signal for corrective action. Failure from political activity is far more likely to persist than failure from market activity. Mistaken political attempts to solve problems created by failure in the marketplace can and often do increase market failure and cause it to continue far longer than would have been the case in the absence of the government solution.

So our emphasis here is not only on the bright side of economic failure but also on the not-so-bright side of political solutions. This emphasis is not an attempt to argue that economic failures are all good and political solutions are all bad. Rather, we believe that it serves a useful purpose in our attempt to unravel the linkages between success and failure in the political economy. For reasons that become clear as our discussion continues, there is a strong tendency, systemic within the political economy, to overestimate the harm of economic failure and the benefit of political solutions. It is a tendency that undermines the benefits that are possible from public policy.

2. The Bright Side of Economic Failure

Economics has been called the dismal science at least since Thomas Malthus published his famous book, *An Essay on the Principle of Population*, in 1798.[1] In that work the Reverend Malthus laid out a truly dismal fate for mankind. Sexual appetite would inevitably cause the population to outstrip the productive capacity of what was then an agrarian economy. The growing hordes of new workers would depress wages toward the subsistence level. Population growth would then be checked by death, sickness, and malnutrition. With the resulting distress and subsequent decline in the population, and thereby in the labor force, wage rates might rise above subsistence, but the gains would be short-lived. Once again, the expanded income base of workers would raise birth and longevity rates. The expanded labor supply would then return wages to the subsistence level. At best, the economy could expect only to tumble from boom to bust, with little in the way of boom and much in the way of bust. Life for workers would amount to little more than alternating episodes of widespread deprivation shifting to some degree of relief and then back to widespread deprivation.

In the Malthusian view of the economy, there was little hope for the masses. There was, therefore, no hope for changing political and economic institutional arrangements in ways that might relieve the hardship associated with failure and poverty. Relief, whether privately or publicly provided, would and could be only temporary. Relief would serve only to ignite sexual appetites and expand the population. The world would be eternally fraught with failure, both at the individual and societal levels.

The Malthusian perspective is truly dismal, but, fortunately, the underlying theory has not been endorsed by history. In general, Malthus failed to anticipate the dramatic increases in productivity in agriculture and industry. In the two centuries since his book

---

[1] Thomas Robert Malthus, *An Essay on the Principle of Population* (New York: Modern Library, 1960).

was published, people have learned to expand production beyond their tendency to expand population, they have developed birth-control technologies, and they have been able to temper their sexual drives when warranted by conditions. Growth and prosperity, as well as the rising cost of having and rearing children, seem to be conducive to birth control.

Malthus viewed people solely as workers, eaters, and babymakers. In his view, people were totally programmed, unable to learn from their circumstances (no matter how wretched), and completely lacking in the necessary drive to improve those circumstances. He did not realize that an expansion in the number of people represented a potential increase in brain power (the very resource that creates creativity and resourcefulness), which is essential for accelerating growth in productivity but is everywhere scarce.

All in all, in Malthus's view, people could not be counted on to learn from their failures and to take constructive action. Rather, he saw them being driven by biological forces into patterns of behavior that were not significantly influenced by economic incentives. Failure, so to speak, was written in the stars, or genes, with future failures being as fully determined as past ones.

Those, like Thomas Malthus, who take a deterministic view of economic history see few benefits in failure. For them, there is no bright side, and the title of this chapter is no more than an contradiction in terms. In choosing this title, however, we do not mean to suggest there is no dark side to failure. There certainly is one, and we devoted much of the first chapter to acknowledging that point in statistical, if not humanistic, terms. At the same time, though, our choice of chapter title is intended to indicate in stark terms the central thesis of the chapter—namely, that there is also a bright side to failure. This bright side must also be acknowledged for what it is and why it exists. Only then can failures, and proposed policy remedies, be properly understood and appreciated.

Scarcity and the Connection between Success and Failure

One essential ingredient in the Malthusian specter is accepted fully by economists, and that is the reality of limits. At all times, the world is beset with limits on what can be accomplished (including how many mouths can be fed). During any period of time, there are only so many resources available for use and only so much that is known about using the available resources to satisfy people's competing interests and desires. As economists since Malthus have never ceased to point out, every economic decision that is made runs up against the reality of scarcity, or people's inability to do everything and have everything they would like.

In simple terms, scarcity means that although people may be able to do much—produce a lot, earn large incomes, and consume a great deal—there are many things they cannot have or do. Such an observation is so obvious that it might be dismissed as trivial. However, the reality of scarcity is commonly overlooked, as evidenced by so many individuals who talk as if they believe that all failures are or should be avoidable. Yet, an understanding of scarcity keenly focuses attention on a fundamental and pervasive cause of failure: people's absolute inability to have everything that is desirable and the pervasive necessity of their making choices.

Failures occur frequently because the successes that are occurring in the economy deny resources to the ventures that fail. When the automobile was invented, many producers of horse-drawn buggies could not continue to operate. Resources were diverted into the production of cars, as buggymakers were no longer able to offer buggies at prices that were attractive to consumers and pay the wages and input prices necessary to compete against automobile producers for resources.

The ensuing failures of the buggy industry in the early part of this century may have appeared to have been caused solely by financial consequences when consumers switched to cars. The revenues of buggy producers, no doubt, decreased when fewer buggies were sold. Costs of buggy production may have risen because of the emerging competition from automobile producers for resources. Buggy producers may have seen their demise as a matter of losses on their accounting statements. Those losses reduced the availability of loans and increased interest rates on loans (or lowered the prices of their stocks), making continued production impossible. But the source of the losses of buggy producers was fundamentally a matter of scarcity and the inability of the economy to expand the production of automobiles while maintaining the same level of production of all other goods and services. Those limitations were merely communicated in stark financial terms to the buggy producers, who found that consumers preferred that scarce productive

17

resources be reallocated from now-less-useful buggies to now-more-useful automobiles.

The reality of scarcity also explains why many farms have had to fold: they were not able to keep up with the competition for land, farm workers, and tractors that farm owners need for continued operations. It explains why steel, tire, shoe, and textile plants have closed as resources have been diverted to other uses. The reality of scarcity also explains why workers are often displaced as other resources in their plants are competed away (diverted to other uses).

However, the reality of scarcity also demonstrates the reality of a bright side to all of the noted failures. The bright side of failure is that something else is accomplished, something else is produced, some other desire is satisfied. Indeed, the reality of scarcity teaches that failure emerges, in part, from achievements of greater importance. Consumers who want automobiles more than buggies get what they want. Automobile producers win in the competitive struggle for consumers, and they win in the competitive struggle for resources. Competition drives up the prices of land, labor, and materials to the point that buggy producers can no longer afford to continue the production of buggies and are doomed to failure.

Seen from the perspective of scarcity, failures might often be viewed as a barometer of what the economy is doing right, not wrong—of the progress that is being made, not lost. Support for this view comes from the fact that, contrary to what most people think, business failures are not primarily a result of weakness in the economy. Recent research by economists Sarah Lane and Martha Schary has shown that there is little connection between business failures and the business cycle. Indeed, during the prosperous years 1985–86, there was a 23 percent increase in U.S. business failures. In summarizing their research, Lane and Schary state:

> Generally, one assumes that an increase in business failures is a sign of weakness in the economy. . . . The assumption is incorrect. . . . [A]n increase in business failures actually may be due to factors implying strength in the economy, such as an increase in the number of new firms. Because younger firms are more likely to fail, the rate of failure will increase. Further, business failures are one method by which the economy retools or redistributes resources so as

to exploit new technology or to produce goods and services in response to changing demands.[2]

Steel and Textiles

To use a classic case study, Nucor Steel—which is based in Charlotte, North Carolina, and operates minimills mainly in the Southeast—has been very successful in meeting market competition. Nucor Steel has expanded and prospered in a U.S. industry that supposedly was on its deathbed in the 1970s.

Nucor has extended its market share by opening mills in the Midwest and by introducing a new and improved method of making structural steel. In doing so, it has contributed to the demise of less competitive steel plants, as well as less competitive firms in industries seemingly unrelated to steel, such as the textile and apparel industry.

According to the textile and apparel industry's political literature, which strongly supported restrictions on textile and apparel imports in the mid-1980s, more than 250 plants were closed and 300,000 workers were displaced in the U.S. industry between 1980 and 1985.[3] The industry blames textile and apparel imports that are produced with cheap foreign labor, which no doubt is partially correct. At the same time, the industry explanation is greatly misleading and incomplete. It doesn't explain why wages paid textile workers are so high in the United States, and why the U.S. textile industry, but not every other industry in textile-producing states, has to shrink. If there were no other uses for the resources that textile firms use, the prices textile manufacturers paid for them would also be cheap because there would be little alternative demand for those resources. Textile workers in this country would be as cheap to hire as workers in other countries. Buildings and machinery owned by textile firms would be equally cheap. Thus, production costs would be no higher here than elsewhere in the world, and domestic textile firms could outcompete foreign imports for American consumer purchases simply because domestic firms

---

[2]See Sarah J. Lane and Martha Schary, "Understanding the Business Failure Rate," *Contemporary Policy Issues* 9 (October 1991): 93–105.

[3]See Ellison S. McKissick, Jr., "Sweatshirts and Sweatshops," *Wall Street Journal*, September 4, 1985, p. 23.

would not have to incur transatlantic and transpacific shipping costs.

The fact is that textile resources have alternative uses, as the reality of scarcity dictates. Those resources also come dear because of their alternative and productive uses. Both here and abroad, many textile plants have failed because of the successes of other domestic textile plants, or progressive firms in other industries such as Nucor Steel, that succeed because they are producing better products at lower costs. An overriding reason for failed textile plants is that the supply of some textile products at times has outstripped the domestic demand for them, depressing their prices to levels that force some domestic firms to fail. A notable characteristic of textile products is that they are fungible, meaning that they are interchangable. Accordingly, domestic textile firms can contribute to the oversupply problem as easily as foreign textile firms, which suggests that the closure of many domestic textile plants is explained as much by domestic as by foreign competition.[4]

Domestic textile firms have also closed because other segments of the domestic economy have expanded, imposing greater demands on the resources that are needed for textile production. Amid all the textile industry clamor denouncing imports as the one cause of closed plants and displaced workers, it is interesting to note that at the time the industry was seeking protection from imports, textile production in the United States was at an all-time high and unemployment rates in textile states had been falling for some time—not exactly what one would expect if the industry were truly in retreat because of imports.

The combination of closed plants and a generally expanding economy indicates that firms that have been forced out of business are the victims of successes in the economy. In short, scarcity ensures that expansions and contractions—successes and failures—go hand in hand and that losses accompany gains.

---

[4]According to econometric research done by one of the authors, a substantial share—more than 80 percent—of the employment losses between 1973 and 1984 in the textile industry (as distinguished from the apparel industry) is attributable to productivity improvements in the domestic textile industry. See Richard B. McKenzie, *The Relative Impact of Productivity Improvements and Imports on Textile and Apparel Employment* (St. Louis: Center for the Study of American Business, Washington University, February 1986).

Reducing Failure by Reducing Success

From the perspective of scarcity, the 60,000-plus business failures in 1990 are easily explained.[5] Almost 650,000 new business corporations (and, no doubt, several times more proprietorships and partnerships) were founded in 1990.[6] That year, hundreds of thousands, if not millions, of existing businesses also expanded. The result was that the competition for resources was fierce, and something had to give; in practical terms, that meant that some firms and people had to fail. Some of the firms that tried to get started never made their first payroll. Other firms that had been making their payroll for decades could no longer generate enough revenue from the sale of their products to cover the cost of resources necessary to produce those products. They literally failed because of the successes of others.

The more successes there are, the more failures there are likely to be. That is a lesson to be learned from the principle of scarcity. Of course, the relationship between success and failure, however measured, is not likely to be one to one. Over time, growth occurs. More resources are discovered. More productive ways of using available resources are developed. Fewer resources are needed to produce more goods and services. At times, some firms that succeed cause the failure of several other firms. At other times, the emergence of dozens, if not hundreds, of small firms causes the demise of a few large firms.

What should be clear is that the one sure means of reducing the failure rate is to reduce the successes spawned in the economy. Although this is an absurd proposal, the recommendations of policymakers for coping with business and personal failure often amount to exactly that—reducing the incidence of economic failures by impairing the chances for economic success. In general, that is achieved by taxing, regulating, or otherwise restraining those who succeed for the benefit of those who fail.

The Relativity of Failure

Admittedly, business failures occur for many reasons: poor management, gross inefficiency, poor product selection and design,

[5]Bureau of the Census, *Statistical Abstract of the United States: 1992* (Washington: Government Printing Office, 1992), p. 531.

[6]Ibid., p. 530.

ineffective marketing strategies, and inappropriate location. But failures are inevitable even if everything is, in a limited sense, done correctly by everyone involved in production. The product may be well designed and have a ready and adequate market, all resources may be employed in the most cost-effective manner, and location and marketing decisions may have been well conceived. Nevertheless, in spite of the firm's attentiveness to doing things right, the firm may fail and its workers may be displaced.

The problem is that failure in the economy, just as in any good horse race, is not simply a matter of failing to meet well-defined and fixed standards of performance that are clearly understood by market participants. Failure is a matter of relative performance— of failing to do better than others, of not having a better product and a more efficient production process, and of not finding a better location. What's more, "better" keeps changing. "Better" is totally elusive and totally dependent upon particular circumstances and subjective tastes. That means that "better" can vary from product to product and location to location.

Fortunately, "better" keeps getting better. Many firms fail because they did not keep up with the competition; they did not continue to improve their products, to reduce their production costs, to lower their prices. The dark side of failure is the misfortune encountered by failing firms and their workers and suppliers when such firms fall behind in the race to continue to improve performance standards. But this fact also points to the bright side of failure, which consists of improvements in products, technologies, and opportunities. The process that produces failures does so by ensuring that scarce resources will tend to be used by those who can use them most productively—those who can imbue them with the greatest value, given the diversity of circumstances across localities, regions, and countries.

Nowhere is the cause of failure more confused than in discussion of international trade. As noted, the textile industry frequently claims that many domestic producers have failed because of imports. As a textile executive wrote in response to a commentary against textile protectionism by one of the authors,[7] "If you find

---

[7]Richard B. McKenzie, "Textile Gripes Are Made of Whole Cloth," *Wall Street Journal*, April 8, 1988, p. 16.

yourself in the area of Augusta, Maine, I would be pleased to arrange for you to visit our facilities to see the most modern, cost effective woolen mill in the U.S.A. . . ., seriously curtailed in the height of its sales season, due to the erosion of our customer base, as a result of unbridled cheap labor in imported garments."[8]

The executive's chief concern was that his firm had done practically everything right (by developing the most efficient woolen mill), but the mill was still failing in the battle to retain its market share. He suggested, by implication, that having developed the most efficient mill, he should be allowed to succeed. The competition he faced from abroad must be unfair because his company did not have access to the same cheap labor pool. He overlooked, however, an important point. His success in capturing the necessary resources to continue production at a high level must ultimately be relative to other producers, not only abroad but in this country.

Other producers in Maine are successful. They are able to fend off foreign competition and attract the needed labor and other required resources. Otherwise, as noted earlier, wages of woolen workers and the prices of other resources in the Augusta area would not be as high as they are. Seen from this perspective, the textile company executive could just as easily blame other producers in his area for his failures as he could the "unbridled cheap labor in imported garments." The executive's firm had to curtail its production and give up its market share to foreign producers because it could not get the resources it needed at competitive prices in Augusta.

Why did the Augusta firm face foreign competition? A complete answer must include full recognition of the fact that international trade is invariably a two-way exchange: Americans get something (imports) from foreigners in exchange for something given up (exports or assets). People in foreign countries have no interest in shipping their goods to the United States without expecting something in return. In fact, they may ship goods to this country with the intent of securing the needed dollars to buy American goods, which they must find attractive—or competitive. Such goods or services that are attractive to foreigners may not be woolen

[8]Personal correspondence.

apparel products, but they may be goods or services that are no less important to other American industries: beef or chicken, farmland, shopping malls, computer programs and designs, insurance services, telecommunication equipment, and thousands of other things.

Naturally, foreigners want to obtain these needed goods in the most cost-effective manner possible. One way of doing so is to improve their relative efficiency in the production of woolen goods and thereby make their imported woolen goods more attractive to American consumers.[9] That is the attribute of competition that concerns the Augusta executive; it is the attribute that he confronts directly—the one most visible in his sales and accounting records.

Nonetheless, the competition is far broader than the executive might believe. His problem is also the result of the foreign demand for other American goods. Foreigners would be totally uninterested in selling woolen goods in U.S. markets if it were not for the other goods they want. In demanding other American goods (which, by the way, are made by "high-wage" American workers), foreigners make sure that something they have is attractive in American markets. To obtain the American goods, they must bid for dollars, and, in doing so, they drive up the value of the dollar on international money markets. The increase in the value of the dollar lowers the price of some foreign goods—for example, woolen goods—in the domestic market until Americans find the prices attractive and are willing to give up the dollar (which foreigners want) to buy the woolen goods.

The foreign demand for American goods has other consequences that are no less important to the fate of the Augusta textile producer. The demand drives up the prices of nonwoolen goods, enabling their producers to attract resources away from domestic woolen producers. The moral of the interactive market process is straightforward. The fate of domestic producers confronting foreign competition can be said to be as much a consequence of domestic competition as it is the result of foreign competition. If nonwoolen producers become more competitive (in terms of productivity, cost,

[9]We do not know what it is that foreigners may find attractive to produce. We use woolen goods as an example because their extensive importation is claimed by the woolen mill executive. All we can really count on is that foreigners will try to find something that they can produce that is attractive to Americans.

quality, and prices) in the domestic and world markets, then the failure of the Augusta woolen firm (and other firms) will be assured. Such woolen firms (and other firms) will have to confront an appreciated dollar, regardless of whether they have the "most modern, most cost effective woolen mill in the U.S.A." That is the way markets work. More fundamentally, though, that is what scarcity and the resulting demands of relative performance dictate.

A surefire means of preventing the contraction, if not the failure, of textile firms—or any other firms—in this country is to stifle competition from abroad by imposing tariffs and quotas on textile imports. But such a policy also stifles domestic competition by preventing nontextile producers from competing resources away from textile producers even though more value can be created for consumers with those resources by the nontextile producers than by the textile producers. The result is not to save jobs, but to save less productive jobs at the expense of more productive jobs.

Furthermore, it must be realized that such a protective policy prevents neither contraction nor failure. It merely redistributes the burden of contraction and failure. Foreigners are not able to secure the dollars they need to buy the amount of American goods they want, causing the contraction, if not failure, of nontextile American firms.

With tariffs and quotas in place, the Augusta woolen mill may be able to outbid other American firms for the supply of available labor and other resources, but that is only another way of shifting the burden of failure. In the process of shifting that burden, however, the national income level will be reduced because total production costs of all goods and services will go up. The economy will then fail to produce the overall improvement in living standard that workers, investors, and consumers presumably want. In other words, a policy of protectionism calms the forces of failure by restraining the forces of success.

Not everyone who concentrates on the failures caused by competition, and wants public policies to protect against those failures, advocates protectionism in the form of import restrictions. Some advocate government bailouts, or special tax breaks, to businesses facing bankruptcy. Many advocate more generous public aid to those who become unemployed or fall into poverty. Others see the solution to economic failure in an industrial policy coordinated at the federal level and designed to ensure that emerging leading-edge industries survive and thrive.

All these responses to failure, however, have one thing in common; to the extent that they reduce some failures, they impose others. Because of scarcity, any government action that eliminates failure by transferring resources to one activity necessarily does so by reducing the resources available to overcome failure in other activities. Unless the incentives contained in the political process will lead to a more efficient allocation of resources than the incentives contained in the marketplace, the result of government attempts to reduce economic failure will themselves be the source of a net increase in that failure. Political incentives seldom outperform market incentives when it comes to prompting decisions that will direct scarce resources into their most productive employments (see chapters 7 and 8).

The Equity of Failure

Failure often treats its victims harshly. For that reason alone, failure in specific instances is something that few individuals can appreciate abstractly, or philosophically. Nonetheless, the broad, philosophical attributes of failure must be acknowledged. In a world of scarcity, the fundamental question is not whether people should accept failure. They have no choice but to accept it. Rather, the question is how far they should go in the attempt to moderate failure through the design of political and economic institutions.

The natural inclination is to reason that institutions should be designed to suppress those attributes of everyday life that people seek to avoid. Accordingly, because most people seek to avoid failure in all their daily dealings, failures should be suppressed, or so it might be reasoned.

Failure means losses in jobs, incomes, and investments. The losses are real, not imagined or solely financial. The business owners who have gone bankrupt or the workers who have been dismissed know in tangible and very personal terms what it means to fail. They are worse off in the particular instances of failures, but that does not mean that they are worse off from the perspective of a social system that permits pervasive failure. Their own private successes may outweigh their private failures, and many of the successes may not have been forthcoming without the failures. (See chapter 4.)

The pervasive failures of many people could be more than balanced by pervasive successes of other people who produce better products at lower costs and prices. Individuals who fail are at the same time gaining from the system that induces people to compete and therefore to fail as well as succeed. In practical terms, that means that the business people who fail may actually be experiencing a higher level of well-being because of the economic system that permits their failure.

Similarly, the workers displaced because their plants shut down suffer a loss of income and security—at the time of displacement. But the loss may only be relative to the income level achieved before displacement, not relative to the income level that would have existed under a different social-political-economic institutional setting that retarded or prevented failures—including job displacement. Whereas the income growth path may be highly irregular under a system that allows unfettered failure, the displaced workers' income path over time may actually be higher and steeper than under some other system in which failures are neither so pervasive nor harsh in their consequences.

"The proof of the pudding is in the eating" is an old adage that applies to failure, at least indirectly. Any system that permits, or even encourages, failures must be judged in terms of what it is intended to do. In the case of the market economy, the test must be in terms of what happens to people's welfare, on balance, over the course of time when many, many opportunities for successes and failures occur. That is why discussions of economic growth, measured by gross national product or national income on a per capita basis over relatively long stretches of time, are so important to the case for the market.[10]

Obviously, there are people in any economy who lose consistently. They go from job to job and eventually drop out of the labor force. They put their savings in stocks, and the market collapses. Their houses burn just after purchase. Their children suffer debilitating illnesses. They may compound their troubles by trying to

[10]See chapters 3 and 4 for a discussion of the importance of failure to economic innovation and growth. See also Milton and Rose Friedman, *Free to Choose: A Personal Statement* (New York: Avon Books, 1981); and Dwight R. Lee and Richard B. McKenzie, *Regulating Government: A Preface to Constitutional Economics* (Lexington, Mass.: Lexington Books, 1987).

drink away their troubles. They and their families end up broke (both financially and physically), homeless, and hopeless. They are complete failures, and their status in life may or may not be their own fault.

The balance between occasional failures and long-run success for such unfortunate people is hardly the type of balance we have had in mind in the foregoing discussion. We would be the first to admit that much of what we have said does not apply to these people, and the fairness of their failure may be seriously questioned. The problem of fairness is a complicated one, and no final resolution will ever be reached on what is and is not fair. (We attempt a systemic discussion of the fairness of failure in chapter 6.)

Concluding Comments

The issues considered in this chapter are sensitive ones. Readers may have continued to wonder throughout how anyone would dare talk about the bright side of a dark topic like failure. We have spoken frankly, devoting little emotion or empathy to those who fail. Our approach and words, however, belie our interests. To repeat, like most of our readers, we are truly concerned with economic hardship. We don't like our own failures (and we both have had them, plenty of them). Bankruptcies, foreclosures, displacement, lost income, declining wealth, and unemployment are not to be pursued for their own sake. Nothing that has been written in this chapter advocates hardship and losses, per se.

Ultimately, our main concern here is with the desirability of alternative political and economic institutions. In addressing the issues of failure, we maintain that failures must be seen for what they are, as part of a wider web of economic activity that takes place within, and is influenced by, the institutional setting. We cannot ignore failures or dismiss them, any more than we can abolish failures. We must assess the potentially productive and constructive roles that failures play in economic interaction and examine how institutional arrangements influence that interaction.

We need to understand, with reasonable clarity, that the sources of failures are not always what many seem to think they are. As in the case of the woolen mill executive, the sources of our failures may be closer to home than we might like to think. Yet, unless such points are appreciated by citizens and policymakers, the remedies proposed will surely exacerbate rather than moderate the problems of failure.

3. Risk, Uncertainty, and Failure

Much formal theorizing about the market economy is based on the model of perfect competition. In this model, all firms are small relative to the market in which they sell, all resources are perfectly mobile, everyone is armed with perfect information, and everyone is a rational economic decisionmaker. In such a world, people never fail in the sense of making a wrong move. No rational person wants to waste valuable resources pursuing objectives that cannot be realized, or that generate less value when more is available, and everyone in the perfectly competitive model has the information to avoid doing so. The emphasis is on outcomes in this model of economic activity, and (not surprisingly, given the assumptions) all outcomes are perfect—at least in the sense that, given the resource and technological constraints, they cannot be improved upon.

Despite the unrealistic assumptions, the model of perfect competition can be useful for obtaining important insights into certain aspects of economic activity. Any attempt to understand something as complex as the economy requires that we simplify our analysis by proceeding from unrealistic assumptions.[1] But, in contrast with the model of perfect competition, our concern here is with the economic process when information is incomplete and mistakes are unavoidable.

As discussed in chapter 2, because of scarcity, failures are endemic to any dynamic economy. In this chapter, we build on this fundamental insight and add another important observation: failures are a product of the scarcity of information about what will happen in markets. More importantly, we conclude that because of limited (or costly) information, the process of expanding people's well-being very likely entails increasing the number of failures—intentionally. In short, increasing income can require more, not fewer, failures.

[1]See Milton Friedman, "The Methodology of Positive Economics," in *Essays in Positive Economics*, ed. Milton Friedman (Chicago: University of Chicago Press, 1958).

The Scarcity of Information

Any assumption regarding perfect information stands at odds with the most fundamental premises of economic analysis. As explained in chapter 2, economists start all their discussions by acknowledging, either explicitly or implicitly, the pervasive scarcity of all resources. Trade-offs abound. Costs in terms of forgoing valuable alternatives are ever present. Perfection is not only unattainable; it is also unsought because even if perfection in one activity were attainable, it would necessitate the loss of too many other things of value from other activities. As Nobel laureate James Buchanan once wrote, summarizing the methods of economists:

> The economists' stock-in-trade—their tools—lies in their ability and proclivity to think about all questions in terms of alternatives. The truth judgment of the moralist, which says that something is wholly right or wholly wrong, is foreign to them. The win-lose, yes-no discussion of politics is not within purview. They do not recognize the either-or, the all-or-nothing, situation as their own. Theirs is not the world of the mutually exclusives. Instead, it is the world of adjustment, of coordinated conflict, of mutual gains.[2]

And so it is with information. There is no more reason to expect people to acquire perfect information, even if it were possible, than there is to expect them to buy the largest and most expensive house that their income (at its limit) would allow. That is true because the cost of acquiring perfect information would be substantial, if not infinite. Far from seeking perfect information, people seek the efficient amount of imperfect information. At some point, acquiring additional information is simply not worth the cost.[3]

Not being able to have everything that they desire, at some point people are unwilling to give up other things just to get more information. For example, they may be unwilling to forgo leisure-time activities (golf) or other goods or services (eating out) just to have more information on a product they are thinking about

---

[2]James M. Buchanan, "Economics and Its Scientific Neighbors," in *The Structure of Economic Science: Essays in Methodology*, ed. Sherman Roy Krupp (Englewood Cliffs, N.J.: Prentice-Hall, 1966), p. 168.

[3]See George J. Stigler, "The Economics of Information," *Journal of Political Economy* 69 (June 1961): 213–25.

purchasing. Beyond some point, people will remain, to a degree, rationally ignorant of what they plan to do, which products they plan to buy, which businesses they plan to start, and what skills they plan to acquire. In other words, just as people do not try to perfect the accomplishment of anything, they should not be expected to perfect the amount of information they acquire.

On one level, failures are assured by rational behavior. As long as people seek less-than-perfect information, they should not be expected to do everything right. People make mistakes. They think they are choosing correctly, whereas they may not be. At times, they buy a product—a drug, for example—that they think is safe and effective. They learn later, however, that although the drug may solve their immediate medical problem (say, lack of sleep), it also causes other medical problems (nervousness, hypertension, or impotence). People buy a franchise to sell a line of cosmetics and then discover that the parent company is in deep financial trouble. They learn a skill (say, how to organize and subsequently administer a foreign-language laboratory) and discover that the skill has been made obsolete (by audio and video language tapes).

The failure that is implied in all of these instances causes economic losses in themselves (scarce resources are involved in each), but that does not mean that it is harmful, on balance. The cost that would have been necessary to avoid failure has not been incurred. To ensure against mistakes and resulting failure would have required costs that were, at least as evaluated before the fact, greater than the cost of failure. Consumers, investors, or workers would have been even worse off if the necessary effort had been expended to acquire enough information to avoid mistakes and failure.

At another level, failures are endemic to the economy because there is absolutely no way that people can absorb more than a very small fraction of the information that ensures their doing everything right. When considered in detail, the production (from inception to use) of even the simplest product requires an immense amount of information. A paper clip, for example, may appear to be a simple product. However, few people know how to make paper clips (at a competitive cost) without relying on many others who know a great deal about manufacturing, packaging, marketing, and distributing them. In obtaining paper clips, people must rely on many (perhaps thousands, if not millions, of) others who collectively harbor all the information needed for paper clip production but who individually do not know all there is to know. The localized information that is possessed in small amounts by each of millions of individuals spread around the globe must somehow be brought together and coordinated, a point that Nobel prize-winning economist Friedrich Hayek has long stressed.[4] There is no reason to expect the process of coordination to be conducted with perfection, simply because no one in the process can be fully informed as to what others can do or want to do with the information they possess. As a consequence of the complexity of the coordinating process (and of rational ignorance), failures are certain. Some people fail and thereby possibly cause a chain reaction of failures. At the same time, much is learned by people in the coordinating process, even though mistakes and failure are endemic to the process.

Failures are produced as one of the inherent benefits of a market seeking to overcome scarcity. People specialize. They focus their talents to increase their productive proficiency, as Adam Smith recognized more than two centuries ago,[5] and then rely on others to provide the many things that they want but do not produce themselves.

The purpose of specialization is to improve people's well-being, but the effect is to divide up the information necessary to do so. As a result, the coordinating problem is magnified and failures proliferate. The resulting failures, however, amount to a loss only as a deduction from an unachievable income level. The income level actually achieved—net of the losses from failures—is still greater than what might have been achieved without benefit of specialization. Of course, fewer failures might be encountered if

---

[4]See Friedrich A. Hayek, "The Use of Knowledge in Society," *American Economic Review* 35 (September 1945); reprinted in Friedrich A. Hayek, *Individualism and Economic Order* (Chicago: University of Chicago Press, 1948).

[5]Adam Smith, *An Inquiry into the Nature and Causes of the Wealth of Nations* (1776; New York: Modern Library, 1937). Smith not only pointed to the advantages of specialization, he was also the first to systematically explain how free-market exchange goes a long way toward coordinating the activities of individuals, each of whom is intent on advancing his own interests with little regard for the interest of others. Accordingly, although failures resulting from imperfect coordination are inevitable if one is to realize the tremendous advantages of specialization, markets serve to minimize those failures. See chapters 4 and 5 for a further discussion of the market's ability to harmonize the diverse interests of self-regarding people.

all people were self-sufficient and if there were no need for coordination—if there were fewer opportunities for mistakes, goofs, mis-
calculations, blunders, boners, misunderstandings, and downright
stupidities. But self-sufficiency would be the biggest blunder of
all in that few people would survive if all attempted to be self-
sufficient; most would quickly find that they were self-insufficient.

The coordinating problem that any economy faces would be relatively simple (but still absolutely difficult) if conditions—broadly
classified as the available resources, technologies, and tastes—were
to remain the same. People could begin to comprehend, albeit
imperfectly, the patterns of relationships as they exist; they could
assume that patterns would be the same in the future, and adjust
their behavior, given their past successes and failures. Even then,
however, coordination would be made difficult by the fact that all
would be adjusting at the same time, and the adjustments would
be made on incomplete information as to how others were adjusting
(and readjusting to account for the adjustments of others).[6]

However, in real-world economies, the coordinating process is
far more difficult because change is practically the only constant
that economies know. A successful economy is one that allows
people to improve their lot, to grow, and to do better in the future
than in the past. Growth and improvement imply changes, and
changes upset many old patterns and relationships. Changes, and
the prospect of more changes, depreciate the value of much past
information, making predictions of future relationships difficult
and tenuous. Consequently, in the presence of change inspired by
the drive for improvement, people must adjust their estimates of
what they should do, or how they should coordinate their actions
with many others who also must adjust to the new realities.

Although there may be regularities in patterns of change, changes
have a general tendency to break down old patterns and foster
new ones. Unfortunately, as noted by economist/social philosopher
Frank Knight, people are plagued with the persistent problem of
conducting their future actions based on perceptions of past regularities. Determining future actions is made extraordinarily complex

[6]An excellent discussion of the coordinating problem, and the role therein of
entrepreneurs, is included in Israel M. Kirzner, *Discovery and the Capitalist Process*
(Chicago: University of Chicago Press, 1985), chaps. 2–4. The importance of entrepreneurs to economic development is the topic of the next chapter in this book.

because the mind is limited in its ability to handle information and because there is so much to know. The world is further complicated by the fact that, as Knight noted, "We do not perceive the present as it is and in its totality, nor do we infer the future from the present with any high degree of dependability, nor yet do we accurately know the consequences of our actions."[7]

In effect, Knight suggested, life is a matter of muddling through, of seeking improvement, and having to confront the many unintended consequences of our actions. Necessary to this process are failures—spawned by change and the coordinating problems that emerge in a far-from-perfect world. In short, the world, as people can understand it, is plagued with uncertainties. People have little advance knowledge of what is going to happen. Uncertainties can then mean failures as well as successes. Uncertainties can be troublesome, if not downright destructive of economic activity. The only recourse is to reduce the prevalence of uncertainties by expanding the amount of information handled. That can be accomplished in part by expanding the number of ventures—that is, by converting future uncertainties into matters of risk, statistically speaking, that allow individuals to anticipate failures and accommodate themselves to the associated costs.

The Risk In Failure

All of life exists on the brink of the future. That statement is obvious, but it helps clarify the problem of coping with failure. Even though people may have lived through the past, they understand only imperfectly what happened to them and to others. They know much about what has happened, but there is also much that they never learned because it was impossible or just too costly to do so. Even if they were given the opportunity to relive the past, there would still be failures (albeit fewer ones) founded on imperfect information and coordination.

Living today with an eye toward the consequences that one's actions may have on one's future welfare is even more problematic, even more fraught with the prospects of failure. That is because one knows, and can know, even less of the future than one knows of the past. If nothing else, people don't have the record of the

[7]Frank H. Knight, *Risk, Uncertainty, and Profit* (Chicago: University of Chicago Press, 1971), p. 202.

future to consult and evaluate. To live "on the brink" literally requires that one makes estimates of observed regularities and project them into the future.[8] Because events are not always identical, and may never again be exactly duplicated, one can project future events only in terms of probabilities. That is to say, if such and such happens, then something with a given probability is likely to follow. In making contingent, highly probabilistic assessments, and acting upon these judgments, one acknowledges the risk that things will not always go as planned. Indeed, one plans on their not going as planned. People recognize the imperfection of categorizing events of the past and drawing associations and making predictions. They also realize that there is much going on in the real world that is beyond their ability to consider. In addition, they realize that individual future outcomes may be totally uncertain, impossible to predict. Their task, therefore, is "to pierce correctly the fog of uncertainty" as best they can, using their powers to reason and to develop appropriate social-economic institutions.[9]

Nevertheless, people's ability to draw associations, as imperfect as it is, enables them to reason that such associations exist in a probabilistic sense. For example, they may know from historical observation that nine out of ten products they develop in a certain category (say, computers) will succeed in the market. Any one of the ten can fail; it's not known which one.[10] But, it is known that for every ten products introduced, one fails, on average. That suggests that the extent of uncertainty can be reduced by extending the range of events in our example to at least ten products. Even then, ten products may not be enough to make certain that the outcome of the venture equals, on average, one failed product out of ten.[11]

---

[8]This is part of what Knight meant when he argued, "It is clear that to live intelligently in our world—that is, to adapt our conduct to future facts—we must use the principle that things similar in some respects will be similar in certain other respects even when they are very different in still other respects." Ibid., p. 206.

[9]Kirzner, p. 53.

[10]It also follows that the cost of the nine successful products must include the losses incurred on the unsuccessful product.

[11]All that probability estimates allow one to say is that the larger the number of products introduced, the more closely will the probability specified be realized: one out of ten will fail. Of the first ten products introduced, chance might have it that three out of ten fail. Of the next ten, none might fail, and so forth until the average of all groupings is one out of ten.

Again, one may not know which products or which plants will be profitable, or which workers will be displaced in which plants, but one does know that if enough products are produced in enough plants, a given percentage will succeed and a given percentage will fail. That means that the cost of the failures can be estimated with tolerable precision. Thus, through a sufficiently large number of events, uncertainty is converted into a known and fixed cost of doing business on par with other normal payments—say, for materials and labor.

Obviously, not all producers, by themselves, are capable of operating on a sufficiently large scale and scope to reduce uncertainty. However, as Frank Knight observed:

> Even if a single producer does not deal with a sufficiently large number of cases of the contingency in question (in a sufficiently short period of time) to secure constancy in effects, the same results may easily be realized, through an organization taking in a large number of producers. This, of course, is the principle of insurance, as familiarly illustrated by the chance of fire loss. No one can say whether a particular building will burn, and most building owners do not operate on a sufficient scale to reduce the loss to constancy (though some do). But as is well known, the effect of insurance is to extend this base to cover operations of a large number of persons and convert the contingency into a fixed cost.[12]

The lesson to be learned is that many failures are, in a restricted but meaningful sense, expected and even planned. People want to deal with a sufficiently large number of cases to reduce or eliminate uncertainty and to convert the costs of production into manageable terms. In the stock market, for example, people try to spread their risk through a variety of stock purchases. The typical stock market investor does not restrict his purchases to one or two stocks. Rather, he assembles a portfolio of stocks, fully aware that some of the stocks will fall in value. The investor will rarely evaluate his entry into the market by the performance of individual stocks, but rather by the performance of his portfolio as a whole. The investor expects, and even plans for, stock failures. To ensure that no stock ever

[12]Knight, p. 213.

falls in value is probably a certain recipe for minimizing the return of the whole portfolio. By assuming the risk of failure, expected income is increased. As a consequence, the investor is better able to buy more stock and is more likely to suffer a greater number of failures because of the greater expected income.

Firm managers and workers also deal with risk and uncertainty through what amounts to a portfolio of activities. Firms produce several products and run several plants knowing that some products will fail and some plants will be closed. In effect, they rationally develop portfolios of products and plants and rationally plan for failures. By developing such portfolios, they expect to increase both the number of failures and their aggregate income.

Similarly, workers and consumers also engage in portfolio management. Workers often develop a variety of skills (or keep their skills general and therefore applicable to many different work environments) and engage in a variety of activities. Many consumers buy appliances, automobiles, and other durable goods that they realize are not of the highest quality, and therefore more likely to fail, but they do so in the anticipation that their portfolios will yield them a greater net return than if they bought a more limited set of more expensive appliances with a lower chance of failure. The important point is that in spite of the failures, consumers and workers manage their personal portfolios with the intent of raising, on balance, their real incomes.

Still, it is not always possible in any category of activities to determine with full accuracy the probability of failure or success. All one may be able to do is develop an estimate of the probability, based on statistical analyses, hunches, educated guesses, and experience. Some uncertainty about probabilities of outcomes will invariably remain in economic activity, if for no other reason than the uniqueness of much economic activity. That is especially true in dynamic economies, in which new situations call for adjustments for which past experience offers little guidance.

Dealing with Uncertainty

"Risk" and "uncertainty" are inexorably linked, both conceptually and practically. They are conceptually linked in that both terms define different states, or degrees, of ignorance. Under risk, the distribution of outcomes for a class of events is known with some degree of precision. As a consequence, the expected value can be computed. (Nine of ten products will succeed and one will fail, for example.) Nevertheless, there is much that may not be completely known. The risk may be only an estimate, more or less roughly made, and the classification system may not include fully identical events, meaning that one may not be completely sure of the exact nature of the loss that will be incurred when, for example, one product fails. Nonetheless, something is known. With risk, there is always the prospect that the potential losses can be covered by insurance.[13]

Under uncertainty, even the distribution of the outcomes is unknown, meaning that one cannot estimate the expected value very well, if at all. That does not mean that nothing is known under conditions of uncertainty. Rather, what is known may not be easily reduced to precise mathematical statements about outcomes.

Most people benefit from the additional information that comes from converting matters of uncertainty to matters of risk. This benefit, like others, is not likely to be costless. Real-world experience (involving successes and failures) is necessary, and this experience is often best learned in the well-known school of hard knocks in which the primary lessons are failures. In this regard, failure is an integral part of the data that ultimately convert an uncertain situation into a risky one. Failure becomes a part of the pattern of outcomes that enables people to assess the risk in a previously uncertain set of circumstances and therefore, with the greater information obtained, make more successful decisions over the long run.

Concluding Comments

If information were not scarce, the case for relying on markets would not be as strong as it is. Markets economize on information. By coordinating the activities of people with diverse interests and skills, the market facilitates the productive specialization that allows people to make maximum use of the information and skills they

---

[13]Even insurance may not be available where there is the potential for "moral hazard," which means, in essence, that the potential insurer can affect significantly the likelihood that the event covered by insurance will occur.

possess. And the failures that markets impose, as well as the successes they bestow, provide informational and motivational signals that create this coordination.

The market also encourages people to acquire information by rewarding them for doing so, within the limits determined by the social value of the information and the social costs of acquiring it. The market also facilitates the acquisition of information by allowing, indeed encouraging, failure. Much valuable information is obtained only by attempting things when the outcomes are highly uncertain and failure is highly probable. Markets encourage people to enter into highly risky ventures by allowing them to reap the reward from those ventures when they succeed. The market ensures that people will make the best use of the information obtained from risky ventures by holding them accountable for the costs of those ventures when they fail.

4. Economic Development, Entrepreneurship, and Failure

Everyone in the economically developed world has benefited from economic growth. A poor person in the United States, for example, is materially better off than the average citizen of an undeveloped country such as Bolivia, Haiti, Poland, China, or Cuba. And the typical middle-class American family has a lifestyle that seems impossibly lavish to the average family in many Third World countries. Economic development has resulted from the innovations that have enabled Americans to produce a bewildering variety of products in large quantities while also giving them more leisure time in which to enjoy those products.

Why is it that some countries have developed while others have not? Any attempt to provide a complete answer to this extremely complicated question would take us far beyond the scope of this book. But an understanding of the economic role of failure is an important step in explaining the conditions that facilitate economic development. Failure is a necessary, though not sufficient, condition for economic development. An economy can generate failures and not develop, as underdeveloped economies obviously do, but an economy that does not experience a large number of failures is an economy that cannot develop.

Tolerating Entrepreneurial Failure

Economic development is critically dependent on what is best described as the entrepreneurial spirit. Without those individuals who can envision what might be and who have the dedication and courage to pursue their visions, few of the technologies and products that have made America's economic development possible would have come into existence. It is easy to forget that when they were first conceived, the technologies and products that are commonplace today were considered by all but the very few to be totally impractical. It is surely the case that if initial support for

43

pursuing entrepreneurial dreams had required a majority vote, Americans today would be living in a very poor world. It is only because individual entrepreneurs have had the freedom to attempt what more "sensible" people would never have attempted that economic development has been possible. Entrepreneurs richly deserve credit for being an indispensable ingredient in economic development.[1]

The important role of entrepreneurial activity in economic progress does not mean that most entrepreneurial ventures contribute to the nation's economic well-being. In fact, quite the opposite is true. It is only a very small percentage of the projects pursued by entrepreneurs that end up adding more to the nation's wealth than they deduct in terms of expended time, talent, and resources. In retrospect, most entrepreneurial ventures turn out to be exactly what most people would have predicted in advance: impractical fantasies. Indeed, it is quite possible to develop a rather unflattering picture of the entrepreneur. Most entrepreneurs can be thought of as differing from other people, not so much in their ability to conceive good ideas as in their ability to become obsessed with the ideas (harebrained or otherwise) they come up with and in their willingness to neglect family, friends, and social conventions in their single-minded efforts to promote those ideas.

This description of the entrepreneur as an inconsiderate crusader is completely consistent with the fact that some entrepreneurs do indeed possess true genius as well as with the fact that some of the ideas of less talented entrepreneurs may turn out to be important, if only by chance. Unfortunately, it is impossible to know in advance which entrepreneurial flights of fancy will result in an economic step forward. The only way to discover the kernel of wheat among all the entrepreneurial chaff is to give all those individuals with an entrepreneurial itch the freedom to thumb their noses at the conventional wisdom and venture forth in hot pursuit of their impossible dreams and improbable schemes.

The freedom to devote resources to innovative quests in the face of daunting odds is a freedom that cannot be tolerated, however, without the discipline of failure. And it cannot be failure with

---

[1]For a good history of the wealth-creating activities of entrepreneurial activity in the United States, see Gerald Gunderson, *The Wealth Creators* (New York: Truman Talley Books, 1989).

forgiveness. The failure has to be sufficiently painful that it cannot be ignored. By his very nature, the entrepreneur whose project is rejected by the consumer will remain convinced that it is the consumer, not his idea, that is mistaken. Unless such brazen entrepreneurial confidence (or stubbornness) is sternly subordinated to consumer preferences, the losses from the many entrepreneurial mistakes would persist and overwhelm the gains from the relatively few entrepreneurial successes. The task that faces any economy that hopes to experience progress is to somehow compare the relative gains to be realized from economic activities that vary from the clearly routine to the apparently ridiculous. Some means has to be devised that gives the entrepreneurial minority both the freedom necessary to be boldly innovative and information on the concerns and evaluations of the more mundane majority, along with the strongest possible incentive to take that information fully into account. Without the discipline of failure to force them to be accountable to the general preferences of the community, entrepreneurial ventures on balance would be economically destructive and entrepreneurial freedom would not—indeed, could not—be tolerated. The economic system that cannot condone failure that accurately reflects economic reality cannot risk freedom, least of all entrepreneurial freedom.

Honest Communication, Cooperation, and Freedom

How can entrepreneurs, as well as resource users in general, best be held accountable to others for the consequences of their activities? Before addressing this question, it is useful to examine a setting that would be ideal from the perspective of accountability. Such a setting is best described as a system of communication that motivates people, both when they succeed and when they fail, to deal with each other with honesty and mutual concern.

An ideal setting for accountability in the use of resources would involve a system of communication that possessed three characteristics. First, it would place all resource users (that is, all people) in constant communication with each other. If the information necessary to direct resources into their most valuable employments is to be available to those in the best position to use it, then each individual needs to receive regular communication regarding the value that others place on the resources that he controls. Second, the ideal communication system would have to somehow ensure that all information is communicated honestly and accurately. The communication of dishonest and inaccurate information on the value derived from resources by different users would impede rather than facilitate efficient resource allocation. Third, when an individual is in communication with others on the relative values they place on marginal units of different resources, he would give their preferences the same weight as he gives his own. In other words, each individual would have the same concern for others as he has for himself. If resources are to be directed into their most productive uses, each individual has to be willing to relinquish resources to those who honestly communicate that they place the highest value on them.

In such a setting, there would be no danger in giving entrepreneurs complete freedom to pursue their most improbable projects. This freedom would be exercised with appropriate attention being given to the costs as well as the benefits of these pursuits. Enormous opportunity for economic progress would thus become possible because of the ability to unleash the type of innovative activity that would be foolish to risk in a setting without the same degree of honest and informed accountability.

The temptation is to dismiss the possibility of such an ideal system of communication as one requiring a level of technological sophistication and moral sensitivity that no sane person could seriously consider possible. Yet, it is possible to achieve a reasonable real-world approximation of such a system. Indeed, a reasonable approximation has been achieved in the form of free-market capitalism. The key to understanding how this approximation is achieved comes from recognizing the incentives established by the general rules of the game that form the basis for economic interaction in free markets. Although these rules are many and can vary somewhat from one free-market setting to another, it is useful to summarize them under the general heading of the "rule of private property."

Under this rule, rights to property are attributes of individuals, with such rights being well defined and subject to transfer only under the condition of mutual consent. This rule brings about a degree of communication that is remarkably like that described as ideal. It does so in three ways.

First, under the rule of private property, people relinquish resources only in return for compensation, normally in the form of a monetary price. Because people typically refuse to sell a resource or product to a potential buyer at one price when others are willing to pay a higher price, the prices that materialize under the rule of private property reflect how much resources are worth, at the margin, to those who place the greatest value on them. These prices are the means by which each market participant communicates to all other market participants the value that he places on the marginal units of resources. Second, there exist strong incentives for people to communicate with each other honestly through market prices. It is to the advantage of market participants to assess carefully and honestly the value they individually realize from an additional unit of each resource and to communicate their desire for more only if the additional unit is worth more to them than the prevailing market price.[2] And this honest response feeds back into the prices of products, which thereby change with changes in preferences and conditions in ways that continue to transmit accurate information on the value that consumers place on products.

Finally, each market participant is primarily concerned with advancing his own objectives, not the objectives of others. But under the rule of private property, he is motivated to act as if he has the same concern for the objectives of others as he has for his own. When an individual reduces his use of a product in response to a higher price, he is saying in effect, "Others are telling me that this product is worth more to them than it is to me, so I will consume less so that they can consume more." Similarly, economic failures such as bankruptcies and unemployment can be thought of as people saying, "Others are telling me that my resources are more valuable in other activities, so I will respond to their preferences by either releasing resources for alternative uses or by shifting to another business venture or job." In a broad sense these failures

---

[2]Although it cannot be denied that under some conditions it is possible for sellers to benefit by overstating the value of their products with excessively high prices, neither can it be denied that this problem is mitigated by market forces. Many special market arrangements exist that reduce the seller's ability to gain from fraud because both sellers and buyers benefit from such arrangements. For a useful discussion of market arrangements of this type, see Benjamin Klein and Keith Leffler, "The Role of Market Forces in Assuring Contractual Performance," *Journal of Political Economy* 89 (August 1981): 615–41.

really reflect the success of free-market capitalism in motivating people to freely, fairly, and honestly cooperate with one another.

Enormous economic productivity and progress is the most obvious feature of free-market capitalism and certainly the feature most discussed by economists. But surely even more important than the wealth that is created under the rule of private property is the individual freedom that the rule allows. When people are abiding by the rule of private property, they can be given a large measure of freedom because they will be held accountable for their actions. Every time that a person—entrepreneur or otherwise—makes use of a resource, he necessarily imposes a cost on others. But when the individual owns the resource in question, he is fully accountable for that cost in that, by using the resource himself, he has to sacrifice the amount that others are willing to pay for it. Given this accountability, there is no harm and much benefit in giving people wide freedom to employ resources as they choose.

The important connection between freedom and the rule of private property can be emphasized by considering instances in which resources are not privately owned. For example, because the atmosphere is not divided up and parceled out as privately owned and controlled property, people are not held accountable through market prices for the costs they impose on others when they use the atmosphere as a dump for automobile exhaust, industrial smoke, toxic fumes, and so on. The result is excessive air pollution and people clamoring for detailed restrictions on individual behavior.[3]

It cannot be overemphasized that the institution of private property protects personal freedom. The reason goes beyond the commonly mentioned fact that private property provides individuals with a sphere of control that is not easily violated by others. In the absence of private property and the accountability that goes with it, there would be widespread sympathy with, and demands for,

---

[3]For useful discussions of the environmental benefits that can be realized by using free-market and private-property approaches to environmental protection, see Garrett Hardin and John A. Baden, *Managing the Commons* (New York: W. H. Freeman, 1977); Richard Stroup and John A. Baden, *Natural Resources: Bureaucratic Myths and Environmental Management* (San Francisco: Pacific Institute for Public Policy Research, 1983); and Terry L. Anderson and Donald R. Leal, *Free Market Environmentalism* (San Francisco: Pacific Research Institute for Public Policy, 1991).

the imposition of controls over a considerable range of individual behavior. It is no mystery why in those countries in which reliance on private property and exchange is officially frowned upon one is most likely to find blatant violations of fundamental human rights and freedoms.

It is also important to emphasize that, as with all general rules, the rule of private property aims at no particular ends. It instead establishes a system of accountability under which people can be left free to pursue their own ends, whatever they may be. The way to evaluate this system is not in terms of particular results, but in terms of how well the process it establishes allows people to interact freely, honestly, and with consideration for others. That does not mean that particular results are unimportant. Rather, the social outcomes that materialize are more likely to be generally advantageous over the long run when people put their trust in rules that establish a process of freedom with accountability. As Friedrich A. Hayek pointed out, "If we knew how freedom would be used, the case for it would largely disappear. . . . Our faith in freedom does not rest on the foreseeable results in particular circumstances but in the belief that it will, on balance, release more forces for the good than for the bad."[4]

It is the long run that is important here. Only by resisting the natural tendency to focus on immediate outcomes and overreact to temporary failures can people hope to realize the long-run economic benefits of freedom with accountability.

Failure as Part of a Bigger Picture

Ultimately, the tolerance for entrepreneurial freedom that is so critical to long-run economic development depends upon public acceptance of the importance of failure in the advancement of an efficient and progressive economy. Such acceptance is possible only when failure is understood as an essential component of a wider pattern of economic progress.

When viewed in isolation, there can be no denying that the consequences of economic failure appear cruel, harsh, and unacceptable. Many hard-working, law-abiding individuals and their

[4]F. A. Hayek, *The Constitution of Liberty* (Chicago: University of Chicago Press, 1960), p. 31.

families experience serious economic hardships under the system of free-market capitalism, and they do so because of events over which they have little or no control. One would have to be callous, insensitive, and completely uninformed to argue that all, or even a significant minority, of the victims of economic failure are getting what they deserve in any particular instance of adversity. But economic outcomes that in isolation seem unacceptable may be the necessary consequence of an economic system that is generating an overall, long-run pattern of outcomes that is completely acceptable and indeed laudable.

The focus on economic failure as being entirely negative results from a tendency that Henry Hazlitt has repeatedly warned against. According to Hazlitt, the major source of error in economic understanding comes from the tendency "to concentrate on . . . short-run effects on special groups and to ignore . . . the long-run effects on the community as a whole."[5] Hazlitt's warning cannot be overemphasized when considering economic failure and the advantages of free-market capitalism. The tendency is to view each failure in isolation, consider only its short-run impact on identifiable individuals, and declare it unacceptable. But to do so is to truncate any attempt at economic understanding. Each failure in a market economy is an inseparable part of a wider web of interactions and outcomes that provides everyone with the maximum opportunity for success in a world of scarcity.

Seeing failure in its broader context is probably more important to public acceptance of entrepreneurial freedom when that freedom leads to successful ventures than when, as most often happens, it leads to failure. It is entrepreneurial success rather than entrepreneurial failure that generates the biggest disruptions and most agonizing failures in the economy. This paradoxical statement is explained by Joseph Schumpeter's description of capitalism as a "process of creative destruction."[6] To Schumpeter, capitalism was a force for revolutionary change. The dynamics of capitalistic

---

[5]See Henry Hazlitt, *Economics in One Lesson* (New York: Arlington House Publishers, 1979), p. 17.

[6]See Joseph Schumpeter, *Capitalism, Socialism and Democracy* (New York: Harper & Row, 1962), pp. 81–86.

growth are characterized by major upheavals in the types of products that people consume and in the ways in which those products are made. In Schumpeter's words:

> In capitalist reality as distinguished from its textbook picture, it is not that kind of competition [price competition] that counts but the competition from the new commodity, the new technology, the new source of supply, the new type of organization (the largest-scale unit of control for instance)—competition which commands a decisive cost or quality advantage and which strikes not at the margins of the profits and the outputs of existing firms but at their very foundations and their very lives.[7]

Schumpeter was describing a rather brutal form of competition. The discovery of improved products, completely new products, and better ways of making existing products means that the value of established products and technologies can fall not just marginally, but precipitously. Those who have committed themselves and their resources to such products and production processes that, through no fault of their own, suddenly become obsolete suffer major declines in wealth as their investments turn sour and their skills become redundant. It is this ruthless failure that is the essence of the free-market process.

It is precisely because of such episodes of economic failure under free-market capitalism that this economic system produces so much success. The Schumpeterian destruction of wealth, which can only be regarded as economic failure when viewed in isolation, is an essential ingredient in the creation of wealth and the economic success of the market process. The loss that some are always suffering in a dynamic market economy reflects a transfer of resources from those who put them to less productive use to those who put them to more productive use, and it presents everyone with a compelling incentive to adapt to changing circumstances in a way that makes the best use of scarce resources. The capitalist process of economic failure through creative destruction is the best hope for the long-run economic progress that is in the best interest of all.

---

[7]Ibid., p. 84.

Concluding Comments

People have always been attracted to economic development and individual freedom. One historical constant is that of people leaving their loved ones, enduring hardships, and risking their lives in the fight for liberty and prosperity. But, as this chapter emphasizes, failure is both a necessary result of, and essential requisite for, economic development and freedom. Unless entrepreneurs have the freedom to pursue risky projects, economic progress will be severely impeded. Yet, although entrepreneurial freedom is necessary for economic progress, it is not all that is needed. Unless entrepreneurs are held accountable for the costs that their resource-using activities impose on the general public, their freedom to strike out in bold new directions will be more a force for waste than for progress and will not be tolerated. And the only effective means of holding entrepreneurial activity, as well as more routine economic activity, accountable is through the stern discipline of failure in the marketplace. The society that cannot condone such failure cannot long condone the type of economic freedom upon which economic progress depends.

5. Freedom and Failure in the Transition to a Market Economy

In a fully developed market economy, condoning failure is not an easy task. It is even more difficult to accept the failure associated with the marketplace and economic freedom in economies, such as those in Eastern Europe and the former Soviet Union, that are attempting to move from a centrally controlled, or socialist, economy to a market economy. Unfortunately, although this fear of failure is understandable, it is the biggest obstacle to the types of bold economic initiative that offer the only hope for socialist economies to begin their transition to a free-market economy. The move from socialism to capitalism provides the most vivid example of the essential role of economic failure in the achievement of economic success.

By any measure of success, socialism has been a failure. Economists from the developed countries are in uncharacteristic agreement when advising socialist countries on what to do about their sick economies. Even those economists who a few years ago were giving advice to socialist bureaucracies on how to do a better job in planning their economies are now recommending market reforms as the only hope for economic development. And there can be little doubt that this advice is correct, at least in broad outline. The source of the sickness in socialist economies is the lack of motivation and information that are generated only when people are free to interact with each other though market exchange. Replacing the coercive and rigid bureaucratic controls of socialism with the incentives and flexibility of markets is advice that has to be heeded if formerly socialist countries are to ever enjoy true prosperity and freedom.

Correct though this advice is, like most advice, it is easy to give but difficult to take. No matter how reform minded the citizens of socialist countries and their leaders may be, the move to a market economy will be difficult and painful. As is often the case with transitions from an undesirable to a desirable situation, the transition from socialism to capitalism is a painful one. If the citizens of socialist countries could begin immediately experiencing the successes and failures of a fully developed market economy, there is little doubt that they would overwhelmingly choose to do so (despite being exposed to decades of propaganda that exaggerated the failures and ignored the successes of capitalism). Yet, there is a widespread reluctance on the part of the victims of socialism to embrace full-fledged economic freedom and market reforms. Their reluctance reflects in large measure the awareness that the transition from socialism to a market economy is a painful transition. There is much fear of the failures that would result from market reform, with much discussion of how to regulate markets to minimize failure. Although such fear is understandable, it is also unfortunate. Those who are trying to throw off the yoke of socialism have more to fear from the failures of freedom in the marketplace than do people in well-established market economies, but unless they overcome their fear, there is little chance that they will be able to make the transition.

Even though the details and difficulties of making the transition vary from one country to another, the general problems associated with the changeover are much the same for all socialist countries. This chapter concentrates on the former Soviet Union because the problems of transition are arguably worse there for the simple reason that market institutions and activity were suppressed for a longer time than they were in Eastern Europe. (In this chapter, for expositional convenience, we refer to the citizens of the republics of the former Soviet Union as Soviets.)

Even though we focus our attention on one (former) country, our discussion is very general in nature. It must be kept in mind that transitions from socialism to capitalism have been attempted only recently and no such attempt has yet been completed, so we are necessarily venturing into uncharted territory. Also, the political structure of the former Soviet Union, and specific reforms being considered and implemented within that structure, have been subject to quick and unpredictable changes. Accordingly, although we believe that economic reform aimed at making the transition from socialism to capitalism will continue in the former Soviet Union, and that it is possible to anticipate some fundamental difficulties this transition has to face, it is not possible to predict the details of the transition with any confidence.

Some Superficial Problems

Several difficulties hampering the transition to a market economy in the former Soviet Union have been discussed extensively.[1] Most of the problems are either overstated or rooted in the more fundamental problem of tolerating the failures that are inherent in any transition from socialism to a market economy.

One perceived problem with Soviet economic reform is what is commonly referred to as the "ruble overhang." Soviet consumers have amassed large holdings of unspent rubles resulting from the rapid growth in the supply of rubles and the fact that there are so few consumer goods available to spend them on. Not being convertible into desirable products, rubles have had little value, which explains a joke—"they pretend to pay us and we pretend to work"—that was so popular among Soviet workers. Although many rubles were confiscated recently in what was officially described as a currency reform, and consumers attempted to spend rubles as rapidly as possible in anticipation of the lifting of price controls, the supply of rubles remains huge. The fear has been that with Soviet consumers allowed to spend all of their money in uncontrolled markets, an explosive inflation will result.[2]

There is also the concern that the Soviet people have never lived in a market economy and therefore lack the mentality necessary to respond appropriately to the incentives of prices and profits. Workers are not used to the disruptions of unemployment and job changes caused by the shifting preferences and improving opportunities in market economies. After decades of depending on the state for subsidized housing, medical care, food, and almost everything else, Soviet consumers are supposedly unprepared to face the full-cost prices and the complex choices of the marketplace.

[1]See, for example, Padma Desai, *Perestroika in Perspective: The Design and Dilemmas of Soviet Reform* (Princeton, N.J.: Princeton University Press, 1990) and Hedrick Smith, *The New Russians* (New York: Random House, 1990).

[2]In fact, the ruble overhang has largely disappeared since price controls on most goods and services were lifted on January 2, 1992.

Furthermore, the entrepreneurial spirit that drives progress in a market economy is seen as almost completely lacking among Soviet citizens.

These concerns, though potentially troublesome in the very short run, are overstated. Privatizing housing and other state-owned assets could soak up the overhang of rubles, in addition to increasing the care given to what is now public property. Of course, temporary price increases are inevitable in a move from state subsidies to private markets, but such one-shot price increases do not constitute inflation. Inflation is a persistent increase in the general price level that is possible only if government allows the money supply to expand more rapidly than the growth in goods and services. Indeed, that was the cause of the tremendous inflation that the Soviet economy suffered under price controls—an inflation that manifested itself in longer lines of shoppers and a steep decline in the market value of the ruble against other currencies. The rapid inflation that has occurred in Russia since the lifting of price controls has resulted from a rapid increase in the money (ruble) supply. Rather than being inflationary, the effect of freeing prices will result in dramatic reductions in the real cost of products to Soviet consumers as market prices bring about significant increases in the quantity and quality of those products.

Also, there can be no doubt that people learn quickly how to respond to the incentives, choices, and opportunities of the marketplace. The populations of such countries as South Korea, Taiwan, and Japan were once assumed by many to lack a market mentality but have demonstrated how quickly such a mentality can arise when people are given the opportunity. When workers find that they are rewarded for greater effort, they make greater effort. When consumers are faced with market prices and abundant alternatives, they quickly learn to make appropriate comparisons and sensible choices. And there is nothing like the potential for profit to stimulate entrepreneurial zeal.[3]

[3]It should be acknowledged, however, that attitudes formed during several generations of socialism can be a barrier to a transition to a market economy. For example, James M. Buchanan argues (for reasons consistent with the argument developed in this chapter) that the attitudes of Soviet citizens are such that they have a difficult time accepting much behavior that is standard in market economies. See James M. Buchanan, "Tacit Presuppositions of Political Economy: Implications for Societies in Transition," Working Paper (Fairfax, Va.: Center for Study of Public Choice, George Mason University, 1991).

The Fear of Freedom

Underlying all the problems associated with a transition from socialism to capitalism is a more fundamental problem that has been almost completely ignored. This problem concerns the interaction between market institutions and the tolerance for freedom that those institutions make possible.

Consider the fact that although most Soviet citizens are anxious for the economic improvements that are now recognized to depend on a market economy, there remains a widespread reluctance among the Soviet people to allow the economic freedom that is charactistic of a market economy. Their reluctance is understandable for the simple reason that in the absence of well-developed market institutions, economic freedom is not the well-disciplined force for economic progress that it is in a well-developed market economy. In an economy lacking market institutions, economic freedom is a disruptive force that generates failures that are difficult to justify as essential to the overall success of market competition. Indeed, in the absence of market institutions, genuine freedom is impossible. Granting people the freedom to pursue their own ends without the discipline of market incentives is not freedom at all, but license in which the undisciplined actions of each extinguishes the freedom of all. Such license is never tolerated for long, and unless it is replaced by the responsible freedom of the marketplace, it is crushed by state repression.

Markets allow freedom to be tolerated because market discipline—imposed in the form of prices, profits, and losses—ensures that people will use their freedom to take the concerns of others into consideration. When this market discipline is taken away, people clamor for a wide range of restrictions on individual choices by government controls.

The suppression of markets was the official policy of the former Soviet government throughout most of its history. Prices existed in the Soviet economy, but they were not prices determined by market transactions. Rather, they were bureaucratically imposed prices that were held far below those levels reflecting the true value of productive inputs and final products. Such administered prices cannot be depended upon to motivate people to employ resources and distribute goods in ways that best consider the diverse demands of dispersed consumers. Given the lack of market-enforced accountability, economic freedom is widely feared even though the alternative is bureaucratically enforced directives that stifle the economy with inflexibility, inertia, and inefficiency.

The resulting fear of freedom in the Soviet economy makes it difficult to move toward a market-based economy in which freedom could be tolerated as a force for a productive economic order. For example, one of former Soviet president Mikhail Gorbachev's few serious attempts at economic reform was to permit the existence of cooperatives—private businesses largely limited to the service sector of the economy and permitted to set their own prices in response to market forces. Predictably, cooperatives were met with much popular resistance, as they were seen correctly as acting without full accountability. Although cooperatives were able to sell their products at market prices, they were able to obtain many of their supplies at controlled prices that did not reflect their full value in alternative employments. That created resentment on the part of those who saw cooperatives profiting by further reducing the availability of chronically scarce subsidized goods that most Soviets had learned to depend upon. So the private-profit-maximizing behavior that is tolerated in market economies prompted public protests—including the destruction of cooperative property—in the Soviet Union.[4] Gorbachev responded to the negative public sentiment by increasing the controls on the cooperatives.

In a well-established market economy, consumers can be tolerant of the freedom of producers to sell their products wherever and to whomever they choose. People recognize that as long as the value they place on an additional unit of a product is at least as great as the value others place on it, they can obtain more of that product. Consumers can be confident that the value they place on products, as reflected in the prices they are willing to pay, are taken fully into consideration by suppliers.

On the other hand, in an economy dominated by state control and at best having only fragmented markets, consumers quite correctly lack such confidence. They grow accustomed to, and dependent upon, mandated allocations of particular goods to local shops. The idea of suppliers having the freedom to desert traditional consumers to make more profitable sales elsewhere is considered intolerable. Not surprisingly, before the Soviet Union split apart, some

[4]See Desai, p. 156.

of its republics outlawed the shipment of goods beyond their borders by local enterprises.[5] The fear in each republic that consumers in other republics would strip their local stores of goods has, if anything, intensified now that the Soviet Union has dissolved into independent republics.[6]

Although unemployment is seldom a welcome prospect to employees, it is an essential feature of any economy that responds appropriately to changing consumer tastes and technological advances. Furthermore, in such a market economy, the freedom of firms to lay off employees can be tolerated because of the opportunities that workers have to relocate to where their skills have the greatest value. Allowing firms the freedom to lay off employees is a far more frightening prospect in the former Soviet Union because workers there do not have the mobility of those who live in market economies. Part of the immobility of Soviet workers is the result of the general intolerance of freedom that pervades nonmarket economies, with government directives rather than market wages serving to allocate labor over alternative employments.

But even though political restrictions on the mobility of Soviet citizens have been eased, the people's mobility is still extremely limited by a chronic shortage of housing. The typical Soviet family considers itself lucky to have an apartment of 500 square feet, and it is not uncommon for two families to share such an apartment. With long queues and the lack of political connections making it almost impossible for a family to obtain housing in another city, being laid off in the city where one has housing is a genuine disaster for most Soviet workers. So, in the absence of a free market in housing, there is little sympathy for the freedom of firms to lay off workers in response to changing market conditions, a freedom that is an essential feature of a productive market economy. In other words, a system that recognizes the freedom only of some economic participants (entrepreneurs, say), but not all of them, is doomed to suffer from a host of problems. Lack of market discipline and accountability is a sign that not everyone's freedom is respected by law. Market discipline and accountability, after all, mean simply

---

[5]See Desai, p. 170.

[6]See Francis X. Clines, "Russia Bars Exit of Its Basic Goods: Trying to Prevent Neighbors from Raiding Its Supplies," *New York Times*, January 11, 1992, p. 1.

that people are free to avoid those who fail to take their interests into account or to compete against them and offer consumers a better deal.

The Dilemma in Making the Transition to the Market

The Soviets' fear of freedom creates a dilemma as they attempt to make the transition from a socialist to a market economy. That dilemma can be stated simply: tolerating freedom is difficult without market institutions, but developing market institutions is impossible without freedom. Fortunately, this dilemma does not have to be a paralyzing one. Market activities and the institutions to facilitate them always exist to some degree, no matter how repressively a government tries to suppress them. No government has ever been successful in eliminating black-market activity and the informal market institutions that arise to facilitate it. As the state liberalizes its policy toward market activity that was formerly illegal, these informal market institutions develop and expand in beneficial ways. So, although allowing people to pursue their own purposes within the legal structures that exist in formerly socialist economies cannot provide the same degree of freedom enjoyed by those who live in established market economies, some degree of freedom is possible. And although that freedom will initially be subjected only to the rudimentary discipline of rudimentary markets, it is a freedom that is necessary for the development of market institutions and more complete freedom.

The republics of the former Soviet Union do not have the basic institutions required for the operation and freedom of a market economy, although such institutions are beginning to show early signs of development. The type of banking system, commercial codes, private-property rights, and accompanying legal structure needed for the transactions and investment that are the lifeblood of the marketplace simply do not exist in the former Soviet Union. Neither is there a stock market, which is essential for the rational allocation of the capital formation that drives economic progress. These economic institutions, along with the political institutions of limited and stable government, are essential features of the social infrastructure that has to be in place if improvements in the physical infrastructure are to be developed and used efficiently.

If it were somehow possible to impose market institutions by government fiat, then the republics of the former Soviet Union would be able to create an economy in which its citizens could begin benefiting immediately from a full measure of economic freedom. Unfortunately, market institutions cannot simply be laid on by political authorities. Rather, they have to emerge through a process of trial and error that requires time and freedom.[7] The creation of a market economy, just as the operation of such an economy, is a spontaneous and evolving process that can only emerge from freedom; the market cannot be created by central direction.

Furthermore, although no economy can prosper without a well-developed system of market institutions, there is no one set of such institutions appropriate for all market economies. Markets are cultural artifacts, and the specific form of market institutions suitable for one market economy may not be suitable for others. Therefore, although the republics of the former Soviet Union can benefit from the general example of the prosperous market economies, even if the authorities in those republics could choose and impose from above (which they cannot) a set of market institutions as they now exist in another country, the result would likely be disappointing.

The unavoidable conclusion is that the transition from a socialist to a market economy is going to be a painful one for the citizens of the former Soviet Union. The freedom that is necessary if markets are to develop is a freedom that is sure to be disruptive until that development is considerably advanced.

Although this conclusion can hardly appeal to those most optimistic about reforming socialist economies, it should not be taken as a counsel of despair. Freedom is always disruptive, even when it is productively disciplined by a well-developed market. And even in the absence of market institutions, freedom is productive if—as is invariably the case of genuine freedom—market institutions emerge from the exercise of it. Economic progress always takes

[7]"To function efficiently, modern market economies rely on institutions and rules established over a century or more." "A Survey of Business in Eastern Europe," *The Economist*, September 21, 1991. For a useful discussion of the evolutionary process by which social institutions, such as those of the market, are created and reformed, see Karen I. Vaughn, "Can Democratic Society Reform Itself?: The Limits of Constructive Change," Center for the Study of Market Processes Working Paper no. 1 (Fairfax, Va.: George Mason University, 1982). Although Vaughn's concern is with democracies, her discussion also highlights important aspects of reform that apply to nondemocratic societies.

time. No economy has ever gone from poverty to prosperity over-night.[8] All market economies have progressed only over significant periods of time, and all have done so through a process that was never smooth or painless. But they did progress.

Market economies have progressed far beyond that which can ever be possible under socialism. After over 70 years of rigid socialist control, it is now clear to all but the most ideologically blinded that prosperity in the former Soviet Union can be achieved only by freeing citizens to develop the type of market economy that allows them to pursue their individual objectives through cooperative exchange with one another. Along the road to free-market prosper-ity, there will undeniably be many economic failures and disrup-tions, and they will be seen by many as a justification to turn away from the unfettered freedom of the marketplace. But the Soviets gave socialism almost 75 years to prove itself a failure. It can be hoped that they will give freedom in the marketplace a small frac-tion of that time to prove itself a success.

Some Lessons to Be Drawn

Three important lessons can be drawn from recognizing that markets have to emerge in the former Soviet Union from the exer-cise of freedom that, until those markets have emerged, is going to be especially difficult to tolerate.

The first lesson is that the major industrialized countries should not attempt to assist the former Soviet Union with financial aid given for the purpose of motivating and easing the transformation of the Soviet economy from socialism to capitalism. Indeed, finan-cial aid would more likely hinder rather than help the Soviets move to a free market. The benefits from making the transition far exceed the costs, but the benefits are a generation or more away, whereas

---

[8]As if disappointed that the partial lifting of price controls did not result in overnight prosperity, the Tass news agency proclaimed, "No miracle has occurred," on January 2, 1992, the very first day that prices were set free in Russia (as reported by Associated Press writer Thomas Ginsberg, and carried in the American press on January 5, 1992). Not only did this bold and long-postponed lifting of price controls exclude many products, but it took place before state stores and firms were privatized. The full advantage of freeing prices cannot be realized until manufactur-ing and distribution are genuinely privatized and the resulting institutional reform establishes residual claimants to the gains from the efficient response to consumers.

the costs are immediate and (as discussed above) significant. Gorbachev, just as all politicians, was far more sensitive to immediate costs than to delayed benefits, which explains why he never initiated serious economic reform. A serious danger is that by artificially propping up the flawed Soviet economy, financial aid would simply allow Russian president Boris Yeltsin, and his counterparts in the newly independent republics (or their successors), to remain cautious in granting the economic freedom required for genuine economic reform. The painful process of moving to a free-market economy was begun in the former Soviet Union only when economic conditions deteriorated to the point where the temporary pain of freedom and reform was less than the permanent pain of the socialist status quo. By artificially easing the pain of socialism, financial aid would be likely to increase the economic agony that can be eliminated only by facing up to harsh economic reality.

A second lesson is that at the fundamental level, economic reform cannot be approached incrementally. The fundamental ingredient in reform is economic freedom, and the sooner the Soviet people are granted a full measure of that freedom, the better. Economic freedom will be painfully disruptive as market institutions are developed, and if a benevolently motivated government knew in advance exactly how particular freedoms would be used, then possibly it could gradually dispense economic freedom in ways that allow for the benefits of freedom while minimizing the disruptions. But governments are seldom motivated by benevolence and never guided by omniscience.

That is not to deny that economic reform itself will be gradual. No matter how immediately or completely economic freedom is granted, the evolution of market institutions and the expansion of economic prosperity will take considerable time.[9] But to recognize that the actual progress of reform will necessarily be piecemeal is not an argument for gradualism on the part of government. The more clear and decisive the policy of economic freedom, the more difficult it will be for the apparatchiks, who continue to infest the

---

[9]In arguing against a "big bang" approach to Soviet economic reform, Desai points out that "even a 'big bang' policy of simultaneous and instant policy announcements will necessarily encounter reality and the rate of effective *implementation* on different components of the package will diverge, yielding piecemeal reform" (emphasis in original). See Desai, p. 182.

huge bureaucracies in the former Soviet Union and have a vested interest in state controls, to derail movement toward a market economy.

A third lesson is that the move to a market economy in the former Soviet Union, or any socialist country, is not primarily a task for government. There is little government can do to facilitate directly a transition from a socialist economy to a market economy. Markets do not arise as a result of government action. Markets arise as a result of the freedom that requires little more from government than getting out of the way of people attempting to better their conditions through productive activity. Therefore, even if the former Soviet government could be depended upon to efficiently use foreign financial aid to promote the transition to a market-based economy, little if any financial aid would be required. The only financial infusions that can be depended upon to promote prosperity in what were the Soviet republics are private investments that will be forthcoming in significant amounts only when the economic role of government is greatly reduced and, as a consequence, market institutions and arrangements are allowed to develop.

Concluding Comments

The most precious thing provided by a market economy is not an abundance of material wealth but freedom. People who have had the good fortune to spend their lives in economies based on markets have difficulty appreciating their freedom for the same reason it is always difficult to appreciate advantages one has never had to do without. Few of those people are aware of how critically their freedom depends upon the institutions of the marketplace. Consequently, people in market economies find it difficult to understand the ambivalence toward freedom felt by those in socialist countries, or the severity of the problems they face in the attempt to move to a market economy.

Compared to the economic failures that Soviet citizens will have to face in making the transition to a successful free-market economy, the failures that people lucky enough to be born into such an economy face are trivial. However, the reaction to economic failure in well-established market economies is no trivial matter. Just as the political reaction to economic failure in socialist countries has delayed the movement toward a market economy, it has also hampered economic performance and productivity in capitalist countries. As long as people focus on the dark side of economic failure and see it as unfair, the dynamics of the democratic political process practically guarantee that government action will increase failure in the name of reducing it. There is a tendency toward counterproductive political responses to failure (see chapters 7, 8, and 9), and possibly the best way to defuse it is to promote a general public awareness of the fundamental fairness of the failure that results in the free market. We now turn our attention to the case for the fairness of failure.

6. The Fairness of Failure

When economists talk about the advantages of the market economy, they typically emphasize the efficiency generated in the marketplace, often glossing over the failures. The market is seen as directing resources into the production of those products that consumers value the most, as indicated by their purchases. To most economists, the ability of well-functioning markets to generate such efficiency is sufficient justification for preferring decentralized market economies over the more centralized alternatives. Even when recognizing that no market economy will or indeed can perform perfectly, most economists still see free markets as more efficient than economic arrangements relying on greater government control.

But what about the fairness of markets? How fair is the distribution of successes and failures within markets? These questions are central to this chapter.

Fairness and Efficiency

Economic efficiency is not independent of the distribution of successes and failures and the resulting distribution of income. The prices of the products that are produced in markets are to a large extent determined by the income distribution that results from producing them. People possess different resources and skills, and the price of these resources and skills depends on what is produced. Those whose productive endowments are particularly useful in the production of highly sought-after goods will have higher incomes than those with skills that are less in demand. And the goods desired by consumers with the greatest incomes will be the goods most sought after in the marketplace.

If incomes were solely the result of effort and skill, it would be easier to say that these incomes were deserved. But even enthusiastic proponents of market economies admit that luck has at least as much to do with one's income in a market setting as effort and

67

skill.[1] As stressed in the previous chapters, individuals who have developed skills and work hard often suffer financial setbacks as a result of economic circumstances over which they have no control. Automobile workers find themselves displaced when an energy crisis causes consumers to shift to small foreign cars. Farmers lose their land because of shifts in worldwide weather patterns or changes in foreign policy that close off important markets for their produce. Retired couples lose their savings when the firms in which they have invested experience reversals or bankruptcy. Economic failures are a constant feature of market competition; they pose a constant threat to the well-being of everyone, affecting the distribution of income in ways that no one can control.

Therefore, to say that the market produces the goods that people value most may be true, but it ignores the issue of the fairness of the underlying distribution of income. If, because of economic failures, the distribution of income generated by markets is considered unfair, then it can be argued that market economies have little to recommend them despite their efficiency.

Economists often dismiss criticism of markets based on the question of fairness as a red herring. They generally believe that, given the morass of diverse opinions and emotional assertions about what is fair, discussions of fairness are futile.

What, for example, is a fair distribution of income? There has been no shortage of suggestions about what the distribution of income should be—that is, the distribution of income that public policy should try to achieve. Economist Lester Thurow, for example, would have an income distribution equal to that which exists for fully employed white males, with the restriction that the minimum family income be no less than half the average family income.[2] For many, a fair distribution would be complete equality if it were not for the practical problems of maintaining productive incentives. Arthur Okun, a highly respected economist who served as the chairman of the President's Council of Economic Advisers in the Johnson administration, stated that "equality in the distribution of

---

[1]Frank Knight argued that the three sources of income are effort, inheritance, and luck, and that the most important of the three is luck. See Frank H. Knight, *Freedom and Reform* (Indianapolis: Liberty Press, 1982), p. 13.

[2]See Lester C. Thurow, *The Zero-Sum Society* (New York: Penguin Books, 1981), p. 211.

incomes (allowing for voluntary leisure as a form of income) . . . would be my ethical preference."[3]

Of course, the practical problems of achieving anything close to complete income equality are overwhelming, as has been recognized by all responsible observers, including Okun. More equality can be realized only at the cost of reduced economic efficiency, and forcing anything close to perfect equality of incomes would impoverish the economy. Even if there were complete agreement about the exact dimensions of this trade-off between equality and efficiency (and such agreement does not exist even among the experts who have studied the issue), widely varying opinions would still remain concerning the degree of income equality because of the widely varying opinions about the fairness of greater income equality.

Despite the difficulty of addressing coherently this issue of economic fairness, we believe it is a mistake for economists to dismiss fairness as not being a legitimate economic concern. Certainly, economists who favor a free-market economy have a stake in the fairness debate. Those who ignore the concerns that people have about the fairness of the market process are ignoring concerns that are likely to be critical in determining the long-run viability of markets and the economic efficiency that flows from them. If the market economy is widely perceived as unfair because it generates unacceptable failure and an unfair distribution of income, this perception results in pressures for political actions that can undermine an economic order based on markets.[4] Concerns over fairness exert far more political influence than do concerns over general economic efficiency (see chapter 7).

It is tempting to conclude that the best way to protect a market economy against the corrosive perception of unfairness is to implement government programs to moderate the harshness of economic

---

[3]See Arthur M. Okun, *Equality and Efficiency: The Big Tradeoff* (Washington: Brookings Institution 1975), p. 47.

[4]James M. Buchanan, the 1986 Nobel laureate in economics, has argued that the institutions of the marketplace must be seen as fair if they are to maintain the public support necessary to guarantee their survival. See James M. Buchanan, *Liberty, Market and the State: Political Economy in the 1980s* (New York: New York University Press, 1985), chap. 13.

failure and to reduce the income inequality resulting from unrestrained market activity.[5] Unfortunately, such attempts to protect the market against the charge of unfairness are not likely to be successful for at least two reasons.

First, as we demonstrate in subsequent chapters, government is severely limited in its ability to assist the poor and reduce income inequality. Government does the most to help those in need when its efforts to do so are modest (see chapter 9). Indeed, the poor receive the greatest benefit from government action when there is little public sympathy for government attempts to help the victims of economic failure.

Second, even if government were capable of moving the income distribution significantly toward equality, and did so, there is no reason to believe that the resulting distribution would be considered fair by market critics. There is little exaggeration in the old saying that if one placed a confirmed social critic in paradise, he would have a dozen nonnegotiable demands before the end of the week.

But the problem here isn't that some individuals are incorrigible complainers. Most people feel that there is plenty to complain about. Rather, the problem is that there is no generally accepted criterion for determining directly whether an economic outcome, like the distribution of income, is fair.

If market economies are to be afforded a reasonable defense against the charge of unfairness, a case for the fairness of markets has to be made by going behind the particular failures and distributional consequences of market interaction. Any productive discussion of the fairness of markets has to focus attention on the rules that govern market interaction and from which observable market outcomes emerge.

We recognize that there will always be those who believe markets are unfair because they feel that particular outcomes of markets are unfair. Our hope is to get people to consider seriously the argument that the only reasonable way to judge the fairness of any economic system is to focus on the rules defining that system rather than only on the particular outcomes generated by the system.

---

[5]No less a proponent of the market than James M. Buchanan has embraced this conclusion. See ibid.

Rules Versus Outcomes

To discuss fairness in a constructive way—in a way that holds promise for reaching widespread agreement on fairness—it is necessary to consider not the outcome of the market process but rather the rules that define that process.

It is useful to consider a hypothetical situation, such as a meeting of the owners of the National Football League teams. How much progress would be made if the issue under discussion were which two teams would play in the Super Bowl and which one would win the game. Each owner would have a different idea of what the outcome should be and would not be bashful about extolling the fairness of that outcome. Some owners would argue that their teams had been suffering from losing seasons long enough and that it would only be fair for them to win for a change. Other owners would argue that their players had worked the hardest during the off-season and deserve to have their efforts rewarded with a winning season. Yet other owners would claim that their teams have the most talented players and that, in fairness, this superior talent should be rewarded with a Super Bowl victory. Clearly, such a discussion would get nowhere; there could be no hope of the owners agreeing on the fairness of any particular outcome.

Yet, a winner of the Super Bowl is determined every year, and there is no rancor among the team owners over the fairness of the result. How do they reach an agreement in a situation involving so many conflicting interests and so many reasons for considering the results unfair? They do so only because the agreement concerns the rules of the game, not the outcomes of the games.

Even though the outcomes of a process cannot be agreed upon in advance, the rules that determine the process can be. Why can people with opposing interests easily agree to a set of rules even though it is impossible for them to agree beforehand on the result of the rules? One important reason is that it is always possible to come up with rules that generate outcomes that cannot be known in advance. Knowing the rules to a game generally provides only very incomplete knowledge about what to expect from any particular play of the game. A large number of factors will come into play in determining a particular outcome, not the least of which is luck. This uncertainty generally adds to the interest of the game defined

71

by the rules. But more importantly, uncertainty makes it more difficult to favor some at the expense of others by rigging the game. Therefore, people with conflicting interests in outcomes can all see the advantage in agreeing on a set of rules that determine outcomes.[6] If the rules of a game determined with complete certainty the outcome of each and every play, then in effect the rules would be rigged and agreement on them would be as impossible as agreement on the outcomes themselves.

Agreement on rules is also relatively easy because rules are durable. Because rules apply under a wide set of possible but unpredictable circumstances, rules are more likely to be judged on the basis of how generally advantageous the emerging outcomes are likely to be. Also, the durability of rules lengthens the time perspective of those who are subject to them. Even if certain individuals believe that their immediate prospects under a given set of rules are poor, they may still agree to the rules because they feel that they will do well under them over the long run. Again, the people's concern is less likely to center on benefits from specific and immediate outcomes, given their current circumstances, and more likely to center on the long-run pattern of outcomes and the general benefits they bestow on people under a wide variety of circumstances.

The example of football team owners being able to reach agreement on the rules that determine the win/lose records actually understates the advantage of concentrating on rules to facilitate agreement. In football, as with most field and parlor games, for every winner there is necessarily a loser—no matter how the outcomes are determined. Games with this characteristic are often referred to as zero-sum games. A more accurate description would be fixed-sum games: there is a fixed sum for winning, and the play of the game has no effect on the size of the sum but merely on the distribution of the sum. Often, however, the total benefits available to a group can be increased when everyone in that group agrees to a set of rules for distributing benefits rather than trying to agree to a predetermined distribution.

---

[6]According to Friedrich A. Hayek, "It is the ignorance of the future outcome which makes possible agreement on rules which serve as common means for a variety of purposes." See Friedrich A. Hayek, *Law, Legislation and Liberty*, vol. 2, *The Mirage of Social Justice* (Chicago: University of Chicago Press, 1976), p. 4.

An economy, for example, in which everyone has somehow agreed to some fixed distribution of national income would be an impoverished economy. Individuals would have little incentive to work harder or incur risk to increase national income. Allowing income distribution to emerge from rules that establish a close connection between the productivity and income of individuals creates incentives for producing a far greater national income and the potential for making everyone better off. When rules are able to increase available benefits, then it becomes even easier to obtain agreement on rules as opposed to the outcomes of those rules. Even if individuals feel they will always do relatively poorly under a set of rules, they may still agree to the rules because they anticipate being absolutely better off under such rules than they would be otherwise.

Of course, there may be disagreement over the rules. Given that reaching agreement on a particular set of outcomes is seldom possible, the choice typically will be between alternative sets of rules, not between rules and outcomes. In the choice between sets of rules, preferred rules are obviously those that generate preferred consequences. But rules cannot be evaluated productively in terms of particular outcomes and the consequences of those outcomes for particular people. Because of the durability of rules and the uncertainty of the particular outcomes that emerge from them, rules must be evaluated in terms of the long-run opportunities they create for a wide variety of people under a wide variety of circumstances. It is this generalized, long-run perspective that makes it possible for people with varying opinions and conflicting interests to move beyond the paralyzing disagreement that inevitably results when they focus on particular outcomes.

It is evident, therefore, that if discussions of fairness are to be more than an exercise in disagreement, the focus of fairness has to be on rules and people's behavior with respect to rules. To be useful the concept of fairness has to be concerned with what it means to have an agreed-upon set of rules and with whether people are behaving in accordance with those rules.[7] The concept of fair

---

[7]According to Friedrich A. Hayek, "Our whole conception of justice rests on the belief that different views about particulars are capable of being settled by the discovery of rules that, once stated, command general assent." See Hayek, *Law, Legislation and Liberty*, p. 15.

play is one that commands widespread—indeed, universal—agreement. Fair play means playing by the accepted rules. The old saying, "It's not whether you win or lose, but how you play the game," is a completely accurate reflection of what is important in evaluating fairness. Particular outcomes may be considered undesirable, but as long as they emerge from adherence to agreed-upon rules, there exists no compelling reason for arguing that the outcomes are unfair (unless, of course, the rules themselves have somehow been rigged to ensure predetermined outcomes with predetermined winners and losers).

Any effort to define fairness in terms of outcomes will label as unfair outcomes resulting from behavior widely recognized as fair. Economist William Baumol, for example, has argued that fairness can be usefully defined in terms of the characteristics of a distribution of commodities; in particular, a fair distribution of commodities is achieved when no person envies another.[8] Economist Randall Holcombe points out the problem with Baumol's definition, and any other definition of fairness based on outcomes, by considering a simple example. Assume, Holcombe states, that one begins with a distribution between two individuals that is fair by Baumol's, or anyone else's, outcome criterion. Next, consider the situation in which one of the individuals pulls a gun on the other and robs him of $100. Compare this with the situation in which the two individuals agree to wager $100 on the flip of a coin. As judged solely by Baumol's criterion, the new distribution in either case is equally unfair in that they both deviate by the same amount from the outcome considered fair. But almost everyone would see the distribution resulting from robbery as unfair because it resulted from one person violating accepted rules of conduct, and almost everyone would see the distribution resulting from the coin flip as fair because it was the result of rules of conduct agreed upon by the affected parties.[9]

It is not the case that all questions of fairness can be resolved by shifting attention toward rules and away from outcomes. People will always have conflicts over fairness, and that would remain the

[8]See William J. Baumol, "Applied Fairness Theory and Rationing Policy," *American Economic Review* 72 (September 1982): 639–51.

[9]See Randall Holcombe, "Applied Fairness Theory: Comment," *American Economic Review* 73 (December 1983): 1153–56.

case even if people could be convinced to discuss fairness primarily in terms of rules.[10] There is always the potential for disagreement over the relative desirability of alternative rules even though the concern is with the long-run benefits people realize in a wide variety of circumstances. That is certainly the case when the discussion is concerned with the fairness of something as complex as an economic system. Many people remain unconvinced that the rules that form the basis of market economies are generally advantageous— despite what we believe to be overwhelming theoretic and empirical evidence that they are. But because concerns over the fairness of failures generated by markets are important concerns, it is important to address them in a reasonable way. And the only reasonable way such a discussion can proceed is by considering the potential of bringing about general acceptance of the rules of the market.

Recognizing the fact that complete agreement on anything is probably impossible, we argue nonetheless that the rules of the market would have a strong attraction to those who somehow found themselves having to choose an economic system with full knowledge of how alternative systems work but with no knowledge of their particular circumstances in the system chosen. To the extent that the case can be made that people would choose a market economy behind such a veil of ignorance, a case is also being made for the fairness of markets.[11] Making this case also requires more than presenting an argument on the general advantages of market arrangements. A case must be made for the general advantages of market arrangements over those of feasible alternative arrangements. (See chapters 8 and 9 for a discussion of the general consequences likely to result when political rules permit the market

[10]The process of trying to convince people to concentrate on rules when discussing fairness may often be thwarted by the formidable obstacle of self-interest. The argument that particular outcomes are unfair, with no attention being paid to the general desirability of the rules that generated them, is often an effective way for particular individuals, or groups, to obtain valuable privileges. Fairness arguments based on outcomes are likely to be effective in a political setting (see chapter 7).

[11]In his well-known book, *The Theory of Justice* (Cambridge, Mass.: Harvard University Press, 1971), John Rawls developed the concept of fairness in terms of the rules that people agree to behind a "veil of ignorance"—that is, with knowledge of how the rules will work in general but without knowledge of how any particular individual will fare under those rules. Also see Geoffrey Brennan and James M. Buchanan, *The Reason of Rules: Constitutional Political Economy* (Cambridge: Cambridge University Press, 1985), chaps. 7 and 8.

process to be superseded by government action for the purpose of moderating the harshness of economic failure and reducing income inequality.)

There is no actual veil of ignorance, of course, and people do not draw up formal agreements pledging to abide by the rules of any particular economic system. But it is reasonable to think of people implicitly agreeing to a set of economic rules. Such implicit agreement comes from participating in the economy and, on balance, benefiting from this participation by virtue of the fact that others are abiding by the same rules.

Although there is no way that we, or anyone else for that matter, can make a completely convincing argument that markets are fair, we hope that people can be convinced to gauge the fairness of markets primarily from the perspective of the rules of markets and the long-run general consequences of these rules. If that happens, then discussion will be elevated above the simplistic tendency to see as unfair the failures that are the inevitable consequences of market action and to then conclude that market economies are themselves unfair.

The Unintended Consequences of the Market

What are society's economic priorities and objectives? American society does not have a set of economic priorities and objectives, at least not in terms of particular outcomes. All Americans, as individuals, have their own economic priorities and objectives, but there is no way they could ever come to an agreement, except in the most general terms, about what society as a whole should attempt to accomplish.

Even if it were somehow possible for everyone to agree on a particular set of economic outcomes (what should be produced and how it should be distributed), a serious problem would remain. It is safe to say that it would be impossible to implement any agreed-upon plan of production and distribution, even if the plan were technologically feasible given the resources and technology base of the economy. The problem is twofold. First, it would be impossible to know how to coordinate the economic activity necessary to produce a given production bundle. Second, even if the knowledge did exist, there would be no feasible way to bring about the specialization and application of effort necessary to carry out the production plan without resorting to forced labor or violating the agreed-upon distribution of output.[12]

The most important insight of economic theory is that far more is accomplished in an economy that does not aim at particular objectives but gives individuals the freedom to pursue their own objectives, whatever they may be and subject only to broad rules of conduct that apply to all. The economic advantages of such freedom are obvious. No one else knows more about an individual's preferences and objectives than that individual. Also, the best way to pursue an objective almost always depends on particular circumstances and conditions that vary from location to location and often from individual to individual. The best way to grow a particular crop can vary in important ways from one location to another. The personality of one's boss or a colleague can have important implications as to the best way for the individual to go about a particular task. Such locationally specific knowledge is far too varied and detailed to be possessed by any but those who have the most intimate contact with local conditions. Indeed, such knowledge often cannot be articulated even by those who possess it, and the only way it can be transmitted is through direct experience. Without making full use of this localized knowledge of objectives and circumstances, no economy can be very productive. Therefore, imposing restrictions on the use of this knowledge to subordinate individual objectives to the achievement of particular social objectives destroys wealth.

But giving people the freedom to use localized knowledge to pursue their own objectives is not enough to guarantee a productive economy. No one can effectively pursue his objectives in isolation. Few people could survive, much less survive in any degree of comfort, if they were required to produce for themselves everything they consume. People's wealth is completely dependent on their

[12]We are referring here to the well-known problems of directing an economy through central planning. Countries attempting to manage economic decisions with central direction are characterized by shoddy consumer goods, chronic shortages, and general economic inefficiency, as well as by repression of basic freedoms. These predictable consequences are the result of the central planner's inadequate knowledge and his inability to motivate the people to make appropriate economic decisions. See Friedrich A. Hayek, *Individualism and Economic Order* (Chicago: University of Chicago Press, 1948), chaps. 7–9; see also Trygve J. B. Hoff, *Economic Calculation in the Socialist Society* (Indianapolis: Liberty Press, 1981).

ability to pursue their objectives indirectly rather than directly; they must be competent in some narrow economic activity and perform that activity in exchange for claims on the specialized efforts of others. Such specialization obviously requires a tremendous degree of coordination and cooperation among people. If the advantages of specialization are to be realized, the activities and objectives of each individual somehow have to be harmonized with those of all other individuals. What is the advantage of giving individuals the freedom to use their specialized knowledge to produce a product that no one wants? What is the advantage of giving individuals the freedom to pursue their own objectives if the products necessary for those pursuits are not available?

The twin economic imperatives of coordinating the activities of individuals and ensuring that individuals have the freedom to use their localized knowledge to pursue their own objectives can be reconciled only in an economy in which general rules of economic behavior are considered more important than the achievement of particular economic outcomes. The success of market economies is explained by the fact that they consist of a framework of general rules that motivate individuals who are intent on pursuing their private objectives to behave in ways that enhance the opportunities for others to do the same. When exercised within the general rules of the market, individual freedom is consistent with a coordinated pattern of behavior that is generally advantageous. But the particular outcomes of the market are largely unintended consequences that emerge from the interaction of individuals pursuing a wide variety of different objectives. Such outcomes can never be known in advance. Many of them will reflect failure. Some will be liked by almost no one, and probably none will be liked by everyone. But political attempts to use direct action to alter market outcomes necessarily require preventing some individuals from fully using their specialized knowledge within the rules that generally apply.[13]

[13]We are not arguing that attempts should never be made to direct or alter market outcomes. Overriding objectives may call for attempts to achieve particular outcomes directly. For example, the objective of caring for those who, because of mental or physical handicaps, are not able to care for themselves is seen by nearly everyone as an overriding goal. The strength of the case for overriding the market, however, depends not only on the importance of the objective but also on the likelihood that the attempt to alter market outcomes will advance rather than retard achievement of that objective. The possibility that political efforts to reduce the consequences of economic failure will be ineffective, or harmful, is a central issue in subsequent chapters.

78

The General Rules of the Market

What are the general rules of conduct that are the foundation of markets and that define the allowable limits of market interaction? Market economies are complicated social arrangements encompassing such institutions as corporations, money and fractional reserve banking, court systems, and government. Many detailed rules constrain the operation of each of these institutions, but because they vary somewhat from one market economy to another, it would be both impossible and unproductive to specify all of them.

In broad outline, however, the rules of the market are easily stated in terms of rights to private property. All market economies are characterized by rules governing the rights and use of property that is predominantly owned and controlled privately. Stated in broad terms, the rules specify that the rights to property are protected by government and transferable on any terms arrived at through mutual consent, and that contractual agreements made in the exchange of property are subject to enforcement. These rules of private property form the basis for the ability of markets to synchronize the behavior of millions of individuals into a pattern of action that promotes the long-run advantage of all.[14] That holds true even though the individuals have different and often conflicting objectives.

No social arrangement will ever achieve perfection in coordinating the activities of consumers and producers, given the immense complexity, volume, and dispersion of the information pertinent to achieving individual objectives, and the pervasive tendency of people to place far more importance on their own concerns than they do the concerns of others. But the difficulty of the task makes the coordination that is achieved through the rules of private property all the more impressive.

The prices that emerge from the voluntary exchanges that occur under the rules of private property allow people to communicate with each other in a way that promotes an amazing degree of productive cooperation (see chapter 4). Market prices reflect the

---

[14]What we have termed the rules of the market were, in slightly different terms, the three fundamental laws of nature as defined by the famous Scottish philosopher David Hume. As stated by Hume, these laws are "that of the stability of possession, of its transference by consent, and of the performance of promises." Cited in Hayek, *Law, Legislation and Liberty*, vol. 2, *The Mirage of Social Justice*, p. 40.

relative values that people place on additional units of the goods being exchanged. These prices are the means by which all market participants communicate their preferences to each other. And each market participant, even when concerned only with realizing his own objectives, is motivated to respond to market information about the preferences of others by adjusting his decisions so as to accommodate those preferences. When people do not respond to market information in ways that best promote the advantages of others, then they find themselves being disadvantaged through economic failure of one type or another. Becoming unemployed, losing the farmland that has been in the family for generations, or watching one's business go bankrupt are painful failures for those who experience them. But such failures are an integral part of the successful cooperation that emerges when people are free to pursue their private advantages within the rules of private property.

The rules of private property hold people accountable to the concerns of others through the device of failure—failure that either motivates individuals to make more productive use of their property or that results in their property being bid away by others who can make more productive use of it. The accountability that only failure and the threat of failure can impose makes possible the wide-ranging economic freedom experienced in market economies (see chapter 5). That freedom is essential to the superior productivity of market economies. Without such freedom, the economy could not benefit fully from the specialized local knowledge, widely dispersed throughout the population, that must be acted on if resources are to be efficiently used in producing that mix of goods that best conforms to consumer preferences. Plentiful natural resources and access to the latest technological advances will do little to facilitate either a high or an improving standard of living if the economy does not allow economic freedom.

Unfortunately, individuals cannot rely on the rules of private property to impose economic accountability without also accepting the failure that is an inherent part of the market process. If one attempts to moderate the consequences of the failure that is an inevitable feature of market interaction, one reduces the accountability of the market and undermines, at least to some extent, the freedom that this accountability makes possible.

But Is It Fair?

We wish to make the case that only by looking at the entire pattern of market outcomes, and the process that generates those outcomes, can the issue of the fairness of the market be intelligently engaged. We contend that when this is done in an informed and impartial manner, one must conclude that markets are not obviously unfair, even if one is reluctant to embrace markets as being fair.[15]

Because of the information, motivation, and accountability that results when people behave in accordance with the rules of private property, a general economic environment is established that increases the opportunity of all to advance their individual objectives. In other words, the rules that define market behavior are rules that, because they can be characterized as being generally beneficial, satisfy a commonly accepted tenet of fairness. If people were somehow to find themselves choosing an economic system behind a veil of ignorance, they would surely see the general productivity and freedom of markets as major advantages over alternative economic systems. Can there be serious doubt about the type of economic system that future generations would prefer if they had a vote on the issue? The superiority of free-market economies over heavily regulated or centrally planned economies in expanding wealth and providing general opportunities would surely appeal to the yet-unborn.

Admittedly, any discussion of how people would choose an economic system behind a veil of ignorance is necessarily conjectural in that all people find themselves in an economic system governed by preexisting rules. Highly suggestive evidence on the attractiveness of markets in a situation roughly similar to that of the veil of ignorance, however, is found in international migratory patterns. International migration is overwhelmingly in the direction of those countries that rely most on private markets to organize economic activity.

Another characteristic of markets relevant to the concern of fairness is the unintended general pattern of market outcomes. Although

---

[15]We reinforce this conclusion in chapters 7, 8, and 9 by examining the political process as a means of increasing fairness through attempts to moderate the failures of the market process.

people are free to pursue their individual objectives, and indeed find their ability to do so enhanced in a market setting, there are no guarantees in a market that any particular objective of an individual will be realized. Any attempt by one person to accomplish a particular goal, whether successful or unsuccessful, will always result in indirect and unintended consequences affecting the ability of others to accomplish their goals. For this reason, the market itself cannot easily be rigged to favor particular outcomes or particular people.[16] Even the individual with superior talent and aptitude for hard work is not guaranteed success in the marketplace. Indeed, extremely talented people often suffer the most spectacular economic failures. Conversely, those who do not possess attributes normally associated with merit can be, and often are, extremely successful in market economies. Just plain luck is often the most important factor in achieving success or avoiding failure in the marketplace. This fact has often been used as a criticism of markets. But the element of luck, which prevents the rules of market interaction from predetermining who will fail and who will succeed, makes it possible for those rules to be generally accepted as fair.

Even if people accept the fairness of markets on a philosophical level, few have the luxury of contemplating things philosophically when involved in their own day-to-day struggles. Each person is far more concerned about whether he is succeeding or failing than whether the rules he is following result in an overall pattern of generally beneficial economic activity. Indeed, the most natural thing in the world is for an individual to justify special personal exemptions from the rules to advance his own particular goals. Even if the market were working perfectly (and no responsible observer would ever argue that that is the case), an individual would always be better off if he could receive special exemption from the rules of the market. But the fact remains that each individual is better off because others are bound by the rules of the market. And although each individual may see virtue in being able to violate those rules when his economic failure is the only alternative, that

---

[16]Through government action, the market can be rigged to some extent in favor of particular outcomes and individuals. That is not a case so much of the market process being rigged, however, as it is of the political process being rigged. And it will be seen in chapter 7 that political efforts to force markets to yield particular outcomes are typically frustrated.

same individual will not see much virtue in exempting everyone from the constraints of market rules. When people suffer losses in markets, they are making a necessary contribution to the working of an economic system that advances the opportunities of all. Each person would prefer protection against failure while continuing to benefit from the contribution that the failures of others make to economic progress. But the fundamental fairness of markets is in not providing anyone with a free ride on the contributions of others. Everyone has to contribute to the general economic prosperity by accepting both the failures and the successes that come his way.

Concluding Comments

Our argument is that market economies have a strong claim for being considered fair despite—or rather, because of—the failures inherent in market competition. There is no justification for dismissing markets as unfair on the basis of particular failures. That is true no matter how unfair the failures may appear to be. Discussing fairness in terms of outcomes, without reference to the process from which the outcomes emerge, is at best an unproductive exercise.

Favoring the market process as the most efficient and equitable means of organizing economic activity is not the same as being hostile to a government role in the economy. To the contrary, government is essential to the proper working of any market economy (see chapter 7). Every economy is a political economy, and it is impossible to understand the market process without also understanding the political process. Indeed, there is no unique market process. Such processes differ depending on the rules of the political process that define the overall political economy of which the market is a part.

It is certainly possible to conceive of rules for a political economy that provide for a market economy and at the same time give authority to the government to cushion the harshness of economic failure by appropriately altering the distribution of income. Such a system is called a mixed economy. Rules for such a political economy could qualify as being fair if they defined a process that people could agree was generally beneficial.

When thinking about how far the rules should go, however, in allowing government to redistribute income, three related considerations should be kept in mind. First, no political process can cushion the effects of economic failure to the extent that many would consider desirable. Second, the political process, like the market process, cannot be depended on to produce specific outcomes such as a particular income distribution. Rather, it generates a general pattern of outcomes that may or may not be consistent with the objectives of reducing the harshness of failure in the marketplace. Third, reliance on the political process to provide protection against failure can quickly become counterproductive. Indeed, as we argue in the following chapters, the greater the public sympathy for government's efforts to assist those suffering from economic failure, the smaller the benefit to those who most need help. Government is able to maximize the assistance it can provide only when what is expected of government is modest.

The case for the fairness of markets is not a case for reducing government assistance to those who have been most hurt by economic failure. Personally, we would like to see the truly unfortunate in our market economy benefit more from government action, not less. It is our view, however, that government is more likely to help those who most need help if there is both a widespread belief that markets are fair and an equally widespread skepticism that government can increase the fairness of the economy by helping directly the victims of economic failure. To present the argument for this view, we next turn to a more detailed discussion of government and the response of the political process to economic failure.

7. The Politics of Failure

Although the rules of private property allow for failure, they do not allow particular individuals or groups to manipulate power to benefit themselves at the expense of others. Rather, they are rules that, when observed, generate both the information and incentives necessary for people to interact cooperatively and productively for the benefit of all. The general benefits that emerge from the market interaction allow the market process, and the failures that inevitably result from market competition, to be considered fair. Unfortunately, and somewhat paradoxically, the general nature of the benefits that are provided by the market process also make it extremely vulnerable to the charge of unfairness. The significance of this vulnerability can best be understood as it relates to a more general paradox: government is necessary if people are to realize the general benefits of the marketplace and, at the same time, government is the greatest threat to those benefits.

The Necessity of Government

Because of the general benefits provided by adhering to the rules of private property, people are collectively made worse off when anyone cheats on the rules. Any one individual, however, can improve his situation by cheating. It is true that the individual who steals, plunders, or fails to honor contractual obligations in order to avoid economic failure (or achieve economic success) will consequently find himself living in a slightly less productive and tolerant society. But the cost will be spread over the entire population, with the cheater bearing such a minuscule portion that he can ignore it with impunity. If all others continue to abide by the rules of the free-market game, the successful cheater can enjoy all of the general advantages of living in a free and productive society while realizing the additional benefits that come from confiscating some of the wealth of others.

If everyone cheats on the rules, of course, the costs in terms of reduced productivity, tolerance, and general social harmony leave everyone worse off. This possibility does nothing, however, to discourage anyone who believes that he can get away with cheating from attempting to do so. Everyone will reason, and quite correctly so, that denying himself the immediate gains from cheating on the rules will do nothing to reduce the cheating of others. Indeed, in a world in which everyone else is engaged in plunder, it would be the height of folly for an individual to follow faithfully the rules and confine himself to productive activity. In the absence of some restraint on those individuals who would violate the rights of others, the process based on the rules of private property will tend to break down. First the few, and then the many, would find it to their personal advantage to infringe on the property rights of their fellows.

The problem being considered here is that of providing what economists refer to as a public good—that is, a good that is equally available to all individuals in the community once it is made available to any one individual in the community. The productive social order that comes from respect for property rights is every bit as much a public good as the classic example of a public good—namely, national defense. But as with any public good, if a productive social order is to be provided, individuals must pay for it. In this case, individual payments take the form of restraint in the face of temptation to benefit by violating the rights of others. Individuals know that they can benefit from the productive social order being paid for by the restraint of others, quite apart from whether or not they restrain themselves. As a consequence, no one is motivated to show restraint. Therefore, one can expect too little respect for private property and a social order far less productive than it could be.

When faced with the desire for valuable public goods, and the frustration of the free-rider problem, individuals typically are willing to pay a reasonable share of the cost—if their willingness is matched by others. Collective agreement has the potential to make everyone better off. However, it is one thing to reach such a collective agreement and another to ensure that people honor it. If collective agreements actually generate benefits, they have to be enforced. Without the power to impose penalties on those who fail to contribute their share to the production of the public good (whether in the form of cash payments or abiding by the rules), shirking and free riding will soon prevail. This public-goods argument provides a justification for government. The institution of government is granted the power to require individuals to contribute to the production of the public good and to impose penalties on those who do not.

Government is granted police power, and it is the legitimate role of government to use this coercive power to enforce society's rules of the game. In this capacity, government performs the role of an impartial referee who knows the rules of the game, observes the play of the participants, and imposes penalties on those who violate the rules. When government is doing its job, those who persist in violating the property rights of others find themselves imprisoned or otherwise prevented from enjoying the full benefits of a free and productive society. That turns the public good provided by respect for private property into what is called a price-excludable public good. Those who do not pay the price are excluded from the benefits. Within this public-goods perspective, incarceration has a justification independent of the standard arguments for punishing lawbreakers; that is, rehabilitation or revenge. Imprisonment serves the same productive function as the walls of a football stadium or the jamming of television signals. It motivates those who want to benefit from a public good to contribute to the provision of that good.

Of course, government is more than just a referee in the economic game. To some extent it must be a participating player as well. Goods other than the social order that result from adherence to general rules of conduct have public-good characteristics. It is through government that members of the community choose which of these goods to finance, how much to spend on them, and whether to produce them in the public or private sector. Government is called upon here to make genuine economic choices and to engage directly in some productive activities.[1] However, government's dual role as referee and participating player in the economic game causes some obvious and difficult problems. Because government possesses coercive power and is expected to use that power,

---

[1]In this regard, James Buchanan distinguishes between what he refers to as the protective state (the referee role of the state) and the productive state (the active economic role of the state). See James M. Buchanan, *The Limits of Liberty: Between Anarchy and Leviathan* (Chicago: University of Chicago Press, 1975), chap. 4.

it is by necessity exempt from certain rules that apply to all other players in the game. For example, government has the power to violate property rights to some degree by forcing citizens to relinquish some of their wealth in the form of taxes. Also, government not only enters into the game under a less restrictive version of the rules than that imposed on other players but must enforce those rules on all players, including government. In any game, government's position of having to judge its own refractions creates temptations that seldom if ever are resisted entirely.[2]

It is true that government is not a single player but a collective body made up of all members of the community. The fact remains, however, that government decisions are ultimately the results of decisions made by individuals acting in their political roles. And in their political roles, individuals coalesce around certain private objectives and are tempted to ignore the general rules of the game when doing so facilitates their achieving those private objectives. Whether acting alone or in a group, individuals find few things easier than justifying those actions that promote their interests.

Government has an essential role to play if society as a whole is to benefit from the freedom and productivity that comes from collectively adhering to the general rules of private property. However, just as government's role requires that it be both referee and player in the economic game, it is also necessary that government be prevented from ignoring the rules that apply to its own actions. But how can citizens be sure that government will be sufficiently diligent in calling infractions against itself, especially as it is controlled by mortals who have a private interest in violating those rules?

The Political Power of the Few

No matter how fair the economic rules of the game are, or how productive the results of those rules are, government can prevent

---

[2]James Madison considered this problem in *The Federalist* no. 10, when he wrote:

> No man is allowed to be a judge in his own cause, because his interest would certainly bias his judgement, and not improbably, corrupt his integrity. With equal, nay with greater reason, a body of men are unfit to be both judges and parties at the same time; yet what are many of the most important acts of legislation, but so many judicial determinations, not indeed concerning the rights of single persons, but concerning the rights of large bodies of citizens? And what are the different classes of legislators but advocates and parties to the causes which they determine?

or at least moderate some of the failures that inevitably occur by using its power to provide preferential treatment to certain individuals or groups. Although such government action can improve the well-being of some people, at least in the short run, it does so by allowing them a free ride on the contributions others are making to the general well-being by obeying the rules. Government's legitimate function is to prevent some from violating the rules that benefit all, but it is exactly this type of unfairness that results when government attempts to protect particular groups against the failures that are the necessary consequence of market competition. What is of real significance (but so difficult to keep in mind) is that attempts by government to prevent particular market outcomes, no matter how justified such attempts may seem when considered in isolation, serve to undermine the general process of free and responsible social interaction that advances the long-run interests of all.

However, the generally beneficial nature of market interaction is not likely be first and foremost in the minds of individuals who find their jobs eliminated and their skills obsolete because of market responses to changing preferences and technologies. Even though such individuals can find other employment, doing so often requires a significant amount of time and expense. Other employment may necessitate their moving away from family and friends and accepting lower salaries than they previously earned. From their own perspective, such problems could be solved best by government interference with the market adjustments that are threatening their jobs and wealth. The government could do that by protecting the industry in which they work against competition, by covering the industry's losses with subsidies or loan guarantees, or by taking over the industry and running it as a nationalized enterprise.

The result of government taking such actions is a reduction in the cooperative communication of the marketplace as consumers are prevented from buying products they would rather have or are forced to buy, through their taxes, products they would not buy voluntarily. To provide special privileges and benefits to a few, the government is in effect violating the rules of private property upon which the general prosperity of the economy depends. It is as if the few, enjoying the general benefits of the game and taking full advantage of their winnings when they have good hands, decide that they will cheat when they have losing hands and are able to get government to support them in their swindle.[3]

It is one thing, of course, for a few to want government to help them with preferential treatment that harms the many; it is another for the many to allow government to provide such preferential treatment. A primary purpose of democratic political institutions is to prevent a minority from abusing the coercive power of government at the expense of the majority. A widespread but unfortunately naive view is that this objective can be realized through representative democracy and majority-rule voting. What this view ignores is the disproportionate political influence possessed by relatively small groups that have a concentrated interest that can be promoted through government action.

Contrary to popular opinion, small groups rather than large groups commonly have the advantage in representative democracies.[4] When an issue is put to direct vote, of course, the position with the largest number of supporters prevails. However, in representative democracies, few issues are decided by direct vote. Instead, voters choose representatives who act as political agents for the interests of their constituents. For most voters, choice of a political candidate is made on the basis of considerations such as appearance, party affiliation, and vague statements on a number of issues. Most voters have little motivation to acquire in-depth information on either the candidates or the policies they advocate. To become politically well informed would be personally costly but would return little in the way of personal benefits.[5] Except for those few who are interested in political issues—those who enjoy

---

[3]Of course, there are some individuals who, for one reason or another, seem to be recipients of chronically losing hands. There may be legitimate reasons for government to assist such individuals through transfer payments or other forms of relief. Our concern here is with government giving preferential treatment to those who are not suffering, and who would not suffer, from chronic poverty in the absence of publicly provided privileges. That concern bears on the ability of government to provide assistance to those whose situation genuinely warrants such assistance, an issue that we examine in the next two chapters.

[4]See Mancur Olson, Jr., *The Logic of Collective Action* (Cambridge, Mass.: Harvard University Press, 1965).

[5]See Anthony Downs, *An Economic Theory of Democracy* (New York: Harper & Row, 1957), chaps. 11–13.

becoming politically informed—the benefits of making an informed choice at the polls are derived from being better able to direct political decisions in ways that promote one's interest. But from the individual's perspective, this benefit is effectively zero because the probability that his vote will be decisive in the outcome of an election is effectively zero. Most individuals, therefore, spend their time becoming informed not on political decisions but on decisions where the choices they make are decisive in determining the outcomes.

Individuals may feel, for example, that decisions on foreign policy, which affect the prospects for war or peace, are far more important than decisions on the type of hair spray or aftershave they use. But most individuals will quite rationally have more information on such consumer goods than on foreign policy issues because their choice of hair spray determines the hair spray they end up with, whereas the choice they make on foreign policy effectively has no influence on foreign policy. The result is that most politicians are elected to office on the basis of their vague commitments to do good, not on the basis of their firm commitments to the details of particular policies.

Once in office, however, politicians are required to make detailed legislative decisions. Depending on how they make those decisions, they can either promote the general objective of economic productivity or cater to the narrow concerns of particular groups. They are certainly motivated to some degree by a desire to serve the public interest (although few of them would qualify as saints in this regard). If everything else is equal, they no doubt put the public interest ahead of narrow special interests. But everything else is seldom equal when a politician is deciding on legislation that promotes the advantage of a small group by reducing the well-being of the general public.

Legislation that would protect a particular industry against competition, for example, can have a significant impact on the job security and income of those employed in that industry. Each individual in the industry has a noticeable stake in such legislation. Also, members of the industry are typically organized through occupational and professional associations and are therefore able to speak in one clear voice in support of the legislation. There can be no misunderstanding by the politicians as to how their vote on the legislation will affect the support, both at the polls and through campaign contributions, of those connected with the industry. On the other hand, even though the costs of legislation reducing competition invariably exceed the benefits created for the special interests, such costs are spread over the entire population. It is the sheer size of the entire population that explains why the public is seldom able effectively to oppose special-interest legislation. Although the cost imposed on the public may be large in aggregate, the cost to each member of the public is small. Only a few people are even aware of the legislation and the cost it imposes on them. An even smaller number see an advantage in opposing the legislation either alone or by attempting to organize opposition in concert with others. So when legislation benefits a few at the expense of the many, the pressure on politicians comes primarily from the few.

The potential for special interests to dominate the broad public interest in representative democracies has long been recognized by serious students of politics and was a prime concern of those who drafted the U.S. Constitution. In *The Federalist* no. 62, James Madison discussed the political advantage "the sagacious, the enterprising, and the moneyed few [have] over the industrious and uninformed mass of the people." Writing almost a century later about the relative political strength of different groups in the political process, Herbert Spencer observed that "A comparatively small body . . ., coherent, having common interests, and acting under central authority, has an immense advantage over an incoherent public which has no settled policy, and can be brought to act unitedly only under strong provocation."[6]

The tendency in representative democracy for government to respond more readily to narrowly focused interests than to the diffused general interest not only has long been discussed but also has been well documented.[7] A growing literature on what has

[6]Quoted in Milton and Rose Friedman, *Free to Choose: A Personal Statement* (New York: Avon Books, 1981), pp. 285–86.

[7]By concentrating on the disproportionate influence of special interests in democracies, we do not mean to imply that it is greater in democracies than in other forms of government. It certainly is not. Indeed, we believe that democratic representation is essential if there is to be any hope that government will respond to the broad interests of the public. But without constraints on government that go beyond those imposed by democratic representation, organized special interests will possess important political advantages over the unorganized public interest.

become known as the private-interest theory of government has developed over the last few decades, and much of this literature has been buttressed by solid empirical work.[8]

Unfairness as a Special-Interest Political Expedient

No one theory, or combination of theories for that matter, can ever capture all the complexity of the political process. Even though the explanation of special-interest influence is quite useful in interpreting and predicting political outcomes, it does not tell the entire story. Consider the following special-interest program suggested to us by our fellow economist and friend Gordon Tullock.[9]

Under this program, which Tullock very much favors, a tax of $1 would be imposed on everyone in the United States and the resulting $255 million would be mailed to Tullock for his personal use. This program has all the characteristics of a successful special-interest program. The benefits generated would be significant, to say the least, and concentrated on a very easily organized group of one (Tullock is quite an organized individual). At the same time, the costs of the program would be so diffused and insignificantly burdensome that no one would be motivated to become actively opposed to it. Nevertheless, the Tullock transfer program will never achieve political lift-off because it lacks an essential ingredient: the plausible pretense that it would promote some worthy public purpose. Despite assurances from Tullock that he would spend the money only in ways that advance worthy social goals, an element of sincerity is missing.

We are making a serious point. For a special-interest program to be politically successful, it must be presented convincingly as a program designed to serve the public interest. No matter how strong the political muscle of the special interest pushing the program, successful special interests always recognize the political advantage—indeed, necessity—of packaging their programs as public-interest proposals. There always is some plausible connection between a politically viable special-interest program and some worthy sounding social objective such as helping the poor, saving family farms, protecting jobs, or providing for the national defense.

[8]For a survey of much of this empirical work, see Robert D. Tollison, "Public Choice and Legislation," *Virginia Law Review* 74 (March 1988): 339–71.

[9]Conversation with Gordon Tullock.

There is probably no better way to grease the political skids than to claim convincingly that the purpose of legislation is to overcome some social unfairness. For this reason, if it is widely perceived that the failures experienced in the marketplace are unfair to those who experience them, the very basis for the long-run success, and indeed the overall fairness, of market capitalism will become the justification for its political destruction. Those who have failed, in concert with those whose interests are tied to government programs justified on the grounds that they assist those who have failed, will take advantage of widespread perception of the unfairness of market failures to enact a host of special-interest protections against market competition. Such protections are incompatible with the proper functioning, and even the long-run viability, of a market economy.

The Low Cost of Political Compassion

Markets are politically vulnerable to the perception of unfairness because of the strong tendency of the democratic process to magnify people's expression of concern for those they feel deserve to be helped. At first thought, that may seem to be a virtue of the democratic process. Unfortunately, people's expression of concern is magnified by a reduction of their sense of responsibility for the consequences of political decisions. The result is political support for government programs even when there is public awareness that the costs of the programs are far in excess of the benefits. Furthermore, there is a strong tendency for the public to believe that the benefits of government programs are far greater than they actually are. As a result, political support is often forthcoming, and sustained, for costly government programs that fail to accomplish their stated objectives.

The key to understanding how the democratic process magnifies people's charitable impulses by diminishing their individual sense of responsibility is found in the simple arithmetic of majority voting. In only a few elections does the number of voters fall below several thousand, and in many the number ranges into the millions. But whether a few thousand voters or tens of millions of voters participate in an election, the probability that a voter will be killed in an auto accident on the way to the polls is greater than the probability that one vote in the election will determine the outcome. The impotence of the individual voter in affecting the outcome of an election has been used to explain why those who do vote tend to be rationally ignorant of the issues and candidates, and why often only a small percentage of those eligible to vote actually do so. Although voter impotence is useful in explaining political ignorance at the polls, it does not explain why so many go to the polls in the first place.

The fact is that people go to the polls for reasons other than influencing political outcomes. Surely an important motivation for participating in the political process by voting is the satisfaction that comes from expressing oneself in favor of things one approves of or in opposition to things one disapproves of. Voting for a favorite candidate, or for the positions the candidate claims to support, provides much the same satisfaction as does cheering for the home team or sending a get-well card to a sick friend. There is no expectation that one's cheering will determine whether the home team wins, or that one's card will determine whether a sick friend recovers. One receives satisfaction from the act of expression associated with cheering or sending a card.[10]

One can assume that there exists a widespread feeling that those who experience economic failure through no apparent fault of their own are suffering unjustly. Obviously, individuals who share this sentiment will find satisfaction in expressing themselves in favor of providing assistance to those who are seen to be victims of cruel market forces. This sense of satisfaction or moral virtue can find expression in private contributions to alleviate the distress of the disadvantaged. But how much is this feeling of moral virtue worth to an individual? How much will that person be willing to give voluntarily to help those who are seen to be deserving? Based on the evidence from private charitable giving, the answer for most people is that they are willing to give some, but not very much (2.7 percent of national income in 1989).[11] The fact that giving a

---

[10]For interesting discussions of the implications of the indecisiveness of an individual vote, see Geoffrey Brennan and James M. Buchanan, "Voter Choice: Evaluating Political Alternatives," *American Behavioral Scientist* 28 (February 1984): 185–201; and Geoffrey Brennan and Loren Lomasky, "Preferences and Voting Behavior: The Impartial Spectator Goes to Washington," *Economic Philosophy* (1985): 189–211.

[11]See Richard B. McKenzie, *Was the Decade of the 1980s a "Decade of Greed"?* (St. Louis: Center for the Study of American Business, Washington University, July 1991).

dollar to help others costs the donor a dollar serves to restrain the demand for the satisfaction that comes from the private expression of generosity.

To understand the effect on voting behavior of the demand for political expressions of generosity, it is useful to consider a hypothetical situation in which an individual is contemplating how to vote on an agricultural support bill (or whether to vote for a politician who supports it), which he knows will increase his taxes by $500 a year if passed. From watching network news, he is convinced that U.S. farmers are being victimized by market forces and he would derive a sense of satisfaction from helping deserving farmers. Although it is doubtful in the extreme that he would write an annual $500 check to a private charity organized to assist poor farmers, he decides to vote in favor of the agricultural support bill. He does so because voting will enable him to obtain a sense of charitable virtue with little regard to the cost, no matter how high that cost may be. True, if the election were to result in a majority favoring the bill, then this individual voter would have to pay his share of the cost, or $500 per year. But even if his share were far in excess of what he would willingly pay to assist farmers, it would not necessarily discourage him from casting a favorable vote for the agricultural support bill.

As perceived by the individual voter, the expected cost of voting in favor of any expensive government program is not his share of the program's cost if it passes, but rather his share of the cost times the probability that his favorable vote will be the decisive vote. This voter-relevant cost is effectively zero because the probability of any one vote being decisive in determining the outcome of an election is effectively zero. Therefore, even if the public sentiment favoring farmers is a mild one, the political process can magnify this sentiment and transform it into a costly government program. Indeed, a program that receives overwhelming support is usually a program that is far more costly than people would have chosen to support if they had been fully accountable for their individual shares of the cost. That is true even for programs known to be fully effective.

How likely is it that government programs that receive strong majority support on the justification that they will reduce the injustices of the marketplace will be successful in doing so? The answer:

not very. Helping poor farmers, for example, takes more than a majority of the voters expressing themselves at the polls as being in favor of helping poor farmers and the government responding by appropriating money. Genuine help requires that programs be conceived, established, and implemented in ways that give efficient assistance to those most needing it. That is no easy task, and it will not likely be accomplished by simply trusting politicians and civil service employees to carry out the wishes of the public as expressed at the polls. Politicians are subject to pressures to respond to the desires of well-organized groups, which may not be—and seldom are—the groups that the public feels are deserving of help. Organized special-interest influence over farm policy can be overcome only if members of the general public follow up their support at the polls by monitoring the agencies that administer the resulting agricultural programs. Voters must make sure that an agricultural support bill accomplishes what they intended it to accomplish.

Unfortunately, this follow-up is far more costly than voting for an expensive program. Having purchased a feeling of compassion and generosity at the polls at little (expected) cost by voting to protect poor farmers against the unfairness of the marketplace, voters then go about their business with little further thought about farm programs. It is not surprising, therefore, that agricultural programs impose enormous costs on the general public, but do little to help those who are the object of the public's concern. By far the greatest percentage of agricultural subsidies go to the biggest and wealthiest farmers, not to the small family farmers who are about to lose their land and who are featured so prominently on the nightly news. During 1986, for example, direct federal payments to farmers amounted to $11.8 billion.[12] Of this amount, approximately 24 percent went to the largest 4 percent of all farms, those with annual sales of $250,000 or more. Only about 7 percent went to the smallest 62 percent of all farms, those with annual sales of $20,000 or less.

[12]The figures in this paragraph were calculated from information in *Economic Indicators of the Farm Sector: Farm Sector Review, 1986* (Washington: Department of Agriculture, Economic Research Service, January 1988), Table 13 (p. 25). For more on the distributional effects of U.S. agricultural programs, see James Bovard, *The Farm Fiasco* (San Francisco: ICS Press, 1989), especially chap. 6 ("Redistribution via Cows"). According to Bovard, "The annual subsidy per American dairy cow exceeds the per capita income of half the population of the world." Ibid., p. 103.

Federal agricultural programs clearly represent a political perversity. The general public is led unwittingly to endorse programs that reduce the general well-being through higher taxes and a less productive economy to transfer additional wealth to a group that on average is already far wealthier than most citizens. Unfortunately, this example of political perversity is not an isolated one. The public's pervasive feelings of compassion lead to broad political support for the exercise of government power that is exploited by narrowly organized interest groups. The hope that government, through democratic decisionmaking, can be kept responsive to the general long-run interests of the public is easily frustrated. Indeed, the only hope of keeping government faithful to its primary task of impartially enforcing the rules that serve the general interest is to restrain government through restrictions on democracy. Once this is recognized, an interesting possibility suggests itself: the public attitude most conducive to effective compassion for the less fortunate is one that finds people restrained in their political expressions of compassion.

A call for restricting democracy and restraining the public's expression of compassion in the name of compassion no doubt will strike many readers as requiring additional justification. We agree, and in the remainder of this chapter and in following chapters, we build on the above discussion of the democratic process to provide that justification.

The General Advantage of Restricting Democracy

Unrestricted democracy, whether direct or representative, is sure to be abused. When the use of government power is completely responsive to majority rule, the path is wide open for people to use political influence to acquire preferential treatment at the expense of others. And this path will be well traveled. The resulting abuse of government is fundamentally inconsistent with the hope that government will enforce impartially the general rules of the game—rules that must be enforced if people are to realize the full benefits of free and productive interaction among the members of society.

The easier it is to use government to enforce the rules of the game selectively by providing special advantages and exemptions to the politically influential, the more people can be expected to employ their talents and resources to acquire political influence.

They will find political activity the best way to promote or maintain their personal well-being as they seek to either capture the wealth of others or to prevent their wealth from being captured by others. In either case, the emphasis is on the redistribution of existing wealth rather than on the creation of new wealth. In addition to reducing the general level of wealth, unrestricted democracy and the unrestrained political activity that results from it tend to undermine individual freedom. The greater the government's role in deciding the distribution of wealth in the economy, the greater the government's control over the choices of individuals. Accountability depends less on the free choices of individuals subject to the general discipline imposed by market competition and more on detailed government regulations determining what people can and cannot do. The result is less individual freedom as government undermines and threatens the private property rights that government is obliged to protect and upon which individual freedom depends.

To realize the advantages of a government responsive to the general interests of its citizens but protective of a broad range of individual rights against the infringement of others, democracy must be restrained. There must be a division between what government can do in response to majority wishes and what government cannot do regardless of the wishes of the majority. This division is almost always somewhat blurred and often is established by procedural limitations on government activity. For example, the government can incarcerate people, even execute them, but few individuals would argue that government should do so in response to majority vote. In civilized democracies, regardless of what the majority may desire, individuals are protected against imprisonment by due process of law, a well-established set of procedures that government must follow before any individual can be found guilty of a crime. Even in cases of less threatening and universally accepted government activity, it is important to temper majority pressures with required procedural restrictions. Raising revenue through taxation is a legitimate function of government, but the majority should not be able to impose a tax on the minority while exempting themselves. People all feel safer subjecting themselves to majority rule knowing that the rule is operating in such a way that when one's neighbors vote to increase taxes, they are voting to increase their own as well.

Similarly, there is no justification for allowing a majority—or even worse, a small but politically influential minority—to exempt itself from rules that it expects government to impose on everyone else. But that is precisely what happens when organized interest groups use political influence to obtain subsidies, preferential tax breaks, and protections against competitive pressures. Such exemptions from the general rules of the marketplace are argued for, of course, on the basis of the injustice of the economic failures that would otherwise result. Unfortunately, if everyone were able to escape the discipline of the marketplace and the failure that it constantly threatens and often delivers, everyone would suffer a reduction in both wealth and freedom. Unless those who want to be exempted from the rules of the marketplace are willing to have the exemption apply to everyone, the exemption should not be granted to anyone except in the most extreme circumstances. Restrictions that make it difficult for government to excuse some from the rules that apply to others often serve to restrict the exercise of majority rule, even though such restrictions are important safeguards of the general well-being.

Constitutions and Public Opinion as Restraints on Government

A political constitution provides democratic government with both the powers to do those things government should do and the restraint to prevent it from doing those things that it should not do.[13] The framing of a political constitution is much like the framing of an agreement on the rules of any game. Rules are being chosen that will remain in operation over an extended period of time, and it is difficult to know in advance how any particular individual or group will fare relative to others under the rules. Therefore, rules should be chosen that are expected to best promote the general welfare. No matter how generally advantageous the rules are, however, circumstances will arise when circumventing the rules will

[13]Indeed, the widespread acceptance of democracy as the most desirable means of making political decisions depends on binding constitutional constraints on democratic decisionmaking. That was pointed out by Hayek when he wrote, "Agreement to submit to the will of the temporary majority on particular issues is based on an understanding that this majority will abide by more general principles laid down before hand by a more comprehensive body." See Friedrich A. Hayek, *The Constitution of Liberty* (Chicago: University of Chicago Press, 1960), p. 180.

mitigate hardship for, and convey benefits on, particular people. But yielding to the temptation to treat each situation as a special case will work to the long-run disadvantage of all. Indeed, constitutional rules are so important because they are barriers to the temptation to focus on the special circumstances of the moment.

Although constitutional restrictions are essential both to moderating the excesses that would be the inevitable consequence of pure democracy and keeping government faithful to the tasks of impartially enforcing general rules, constitutions by no means provide an assured route to responsible government. The effectiveness of a constitution, no matter how sound the political theory upon which it is based, depends on more than the words that are written on parchment. The U.S. Constitution, without doubt the most effective and durable written constitution in history, has served as a model for numerous political regimes around the world, sometimes being copied almost verbatim. But few such clones have been particularly durable or effective in controlling government. To be successful a constitution has to be derived from and sustained by customs, beliefs, and understandings that are widely accepted within the relevant community. A constitution can guard effectively against only those abuses of government power that are widely recognized as abuses. If prevailing public opinion favors a particular government practice, then constitutional barriers to that practice will soon be breached.

Constitutions are important. They are shaped by public opinion, and they help shape public opinion, on the proper role of government. But a constitution cannot bear the full burden of protecting citizens against the tendency of government to cater to the demands of organized interest groups by reducing the well-being of the general public. A free, productive, and just social order will not long survive the absence of effective constitutional limits on government's proclivity to push for particular outcomes (in the name of fairness) by providing selective exemptions to general rules. And constitutional limits on government will not long remain effective in the absence of public approval of those limits.

Unfortunately, maintaining public approval for limits on government is not an easy task. Somewhat ironically, the public tends to see the market process as unfair for the very reason that the market process promotes the general well-being. And the political process is commonly seen as fair for the very reason that it reduces the general well-being through the granting of special-interest privileges. The general advantage realized from the market process derives from the fact that the market holds people accountable for the costs of their actions. Indeed, the market highlights those costs by concentrating them in ways that make them impossible to ignore. But the public sees this accountability, which often shows up as particular cases of economic failure, as a flaw that justifies government action. On the other hand, the general wealth of the community is reduced because the political process allows people to capture benefits without being accountable for the costs of these benefits. Political action is typically motivated by the opportunity of obtaining concentrated benefits while spreading the costs over the general public. Because these benefits are concentrated, they are highly visible; and because the costs are spread, they tend to go unnoticed. The tendency, then, is for the benefits provided by a particular government action to be highlighted and appreciated, while the costs of that action are obscured and ignored.

The public can all too easily get the impression that the marketplace is full of abuses and that government is the appropriate means for addressing those abuses. Organized groups have a strong motivation to encourage this view when attempting to obtain special-interest advantages through government programs. The special-interest pressure will be almost uniformly in the direction of expanding the scope of government at the expense of reducing the scope of the market.

The only hope for resisting the special-interest pressures that are working to undermine the general advantages of limiting government is a public that is unsympathetic to the use of the political process to obtain protection against failure in the marketplace. If public sympathy for the plight of those who have suffered failure in the marketplace extends to sympathy for bending the rules to provide selective benefits for those who have failed, then it becomes almost impossible for politicians not to bend the rules. And once politicians begin providing exemptions to the general rules to promote particular outcomes demanded by organized interests, the efficiency, freedom, and fairness of the market economy begin to unravel.

The admonition here is not to be unsympathetic to those who have suffered economic failure. Rather, it is to be unsympathetic to government attempts to protect people against economic failure by selectively altering the rules in favor of those experiencing failure. It is one thing for sympathetic family, friends, and private organizations to extend help to those who are suffering hardship. It is quite another thing for government to be sympathetic by allowing those who claim hardship to violate the rules that were designed to benefit all when generally enforced. The best protection against the erosion of the market process—which serves the long-run interest of all citizens—is a public attitude that views with skepticism those who attempt to use government to obtain special privileges.

Concluding Comments

Many readers who have followed our argument to this point no doubt are thinking that they would be willing to live in a society somewhat less productive than it might otherwise be so as to have government programs that make exceptions to the rules of the marketplace to help those who are truly disadvantaged. While recognizing this sentiment as a defensible one if such government programs actually helped the truly disadvantaged, we are not convinced that that is the case. Indeed, we believe that government would do more for those who are most deserving of help if government were severely limited by public skepticism toward its efforts to assist those who have suffered failure in the marketplace. By examining the tendency for organized special interests to dominate the general interest in the political process, we have laid the foundation in this chapter for our view that a limited government is a more compassionate government. We now build on this foundation by considering attempts to help those who have failed badly—the poor—by expanding the power of government to transfer income. The effect of those attempts lends support to the model of government developed in this chapter and to the view that the best hope for a compassionate government lies with public opinion that is skeptical of government attempts to be compassionate.

8. The Failure of Politics?

Can government help the poor? And if it can, what are the limits on the help it can provide, and what is the best way for it to provide that help? In addressing these questions, we build upon the idea (as developed in the previous chapter) that government should not be seen—as it often is—as a monolithic entity with a clear set of social objectives and with the ability to achieve those objectives. Rather, it should be seen as being defined by a set of rules and procedures within which individuals and groups, with diverse objectives and interests, interact for the purpose of promoting their own objectives and interests.

According to the monolithic-entity view, if government fails to achieve an important social objective, such as helping the poor, its failure can be overcome by putting political leaders in power who are sufficiently committed to the objective and by providing them with better information on how to achieve it. On the other hand, in the view of government that informs our discussion, no matter how committed and informed political leaders are, their ability to achieve particular objectives is severely limited by a host of competing interests to which they have to respond if they are to remain political leaders. Accordingly, outcomes tend to emerge from a process of political competition, with it being unlikely that any individual, interest group, or political leader would have chosen those outcomes if they had the power to do so.

Before developing further our view of government as a nexus of competing interests and examining the implications for government's ability to assist those in poverty, we emphasize again that in a broad sense government can help the poor by adjudicating conflicts, protecting citizens against foreign invasion, providing an adequate infrastructure, and enforcing the general rules of the market (see chapters 5 and 6). Those functions help create an environment in which individuals are able to interact productively. The resulting pattern of specialization and exchange encourages each individual to direct his wealth to potentially lucrative activities that expand the opportunities for others to increase their wealth. In the absence of government, achieving such a productive interaction would be highly problematic, and extreme deprivation and poverty would be the norm instead of the rare exception (see chapter 7). Therefore, the single most effective government poverty program consists of government doing nothing more than establishing an environment that facilitates market exchanges. Nothing else that can be done by government comes even remotely close to reducing poverty as much, especially over the long run.

But no matter how faithfully government carries out its limited role of market facilitator, or how successful the market is at creating wealth, poverty will remain. The market rewards individuals on the basis of how well they compete against each other for jobs, market share, cheaper sources of supply, and improved productive techniques—in other words, how well they compete for success in the marketplace. The skills and talents that determine the success of individuals in market competition are unevenly distributed over the population, and so the rewards from market competition are also unevenly distributed. Some people reap enormous incomes while others, lacking even basic skills, earn little if anything. With market rewards unevenly distributed, there will always be poverty in the relative sense if a nation relies entirely on market forces to determine incomes. With some people lacking even the most rudimentary ability to compete, there will doubtless be cases of absolute poverty as well.

An Overview of the Difficulties

Because nearly everyone is aware of the income inequality resulting from market competition, there exists little sentiment for relying solely on the government's ability to establish a productive market setting to alleviate poverty. A rising tide of economic productivity will not lift all boats out of the sea of poverty if some are on the bottom because they lack the ability to float. It is accepted almost universally that government should take direct action to alter the income distribution in favor of the poor.

Implicit in the view that government should alter the income distribution in favor of the poor is the assumption that government actually can alter income distribution in favor of the poor. This assumption is seldom questioned, and it is accepted as obvious that granting government the power to transfer wealth for the express purpose of reducing the inequality of income is an effective way of helping the poor.[1] There are reasons for believing, however, that government can do little to alter the distribution of income and that what government can do to help the poor directly is necessarily modest. Indeed, the point is quickly reached where expanding government for the purpose of helping the poor will leave the poor worse off. Unfortunately, for the same reason that government's ability to assist the poor is limited, a persistent tendency exists for government to expand its activities in the name of reducing income inequality beyond the point where such activities help the poor.

A fundamental limitation on the ability of government to improve the well-being of the poor by transferring income to them derives from the fact that government action always has an effect on how people behave. That government action affects behavior is obvious, and the rationale for many poverty programs is based on the hope that such programs will change the behavior of the poor. When people who would otherwise do without are given adequate amounts of food, clothing, shelter, and medical care, it is hoped that they will be able to develop the skills necessary to provide some minimum standard of living for themselves. Whether poor people who receive transfers from government will take advantage of them to improve their ability to become self-sufficient or take advantage of them by becoming increasingly dependent is a question that has long been a much studied and debated aspect of public policy. What is clear, however, is that unless transfer programs are designed and implemented with the utmost care, they will reduce, at least to some extent, the incentive that recipients have to engage in income-earning activities. Programs that are successful at transferring income to the poor necessarily reduce the cost of being poor.

---

[1]By virtue of carrying out any function, whether providing national defense or maintaining a judicial system, government necessarily takes wealth from some in the form of taxes and transfers it to others as payment for services rendered. But these transfers are incidental to the government activity and are not intended to alter the distribution of income in any systematic way.

The ability of transfer programs to help the poor is also affected in important ways by the reactions of the nonpoor to those programs. Transfer programs require imposing a tax burden on those who are saving, investing, and working. Most, though certainly not all, of the burden falls on the nonpoor, who respond by saving, investing, and working less than they otherwise would. The effect of the disincentives caused by taxes to finance transfers has been studied and debated extensively. Although there is no consensus on the exact magnitude of the productivity effect of such taxes, there is no doubt that it is negative. The result of financing transfers to the poor is a reduction in economic growth and productivity, which means the income slice that goes to the poor comes out of a smaller economic pie.

Another potentially important but less studied response of the nonpoor to government transfer payments to the poor concerns private charitable contributions. People contribute to private charities for a variety of reasons, but certainly one is the desire to help those who would otherwise be destitute. There can be little doubt that the motivation to make private contributions to charitable organizations is reduced if it is felt that much of the poverty problem has already been taken care of through government programs financed by taxes. Again, there may not be agreement as to how much public transfers displace private transfers, but there can be little doubt that such displacement does take place and that it reduces the ability of government to help the poor.

Finally, the political behavior of people is affected by government transfer payments to the poor in ways that erode the benefits the poor realize from those payments. Government transfers are not made in a political vacuum. People who want government programs to aid those at the bottom of the income distribution find that, to obtain the necessary political support, they have to support programs that others are anxious to have funded. Out of this legislative logrolling emerges a host of government transfer programs dispersing benefits to a host of different interest groups, with the poor being only one of many. That not only reduces the amount of funding devoted to reducing poverty but also forces the the poor to pay some portion of the cost of government programs benefiting the nonpoor, either directly through tax payments or indirectly through a less productive economy.

The political response to transfer programs and its effect on the ability of government to reduce poverty has received very little consideration in most discussions of political efforts to help the poor. Our feeling, however, is that the difficulty of reducing poverty through government transfers cannot be understood fully without focusing attention on the politics of transfers, and a primary objective of this chapter and the next one is to do just that. Before we turn to the politics of government transfers, however, there is value in restating and clarifying points central to our discussion of the private responses to government attempts to help the poor.

Private Responses to Government Transfers to the Poor

Government transfer programs elicit different responses from recipients and donors. Yet both kinds of responses work to undermine the programs.

The Response of Recipients

It is hard to imagine designing a transfer program to reduce poverty that does not reduce the incentives of the poor to overcome poverty by engaging in productive activity. If a transfer program is to provide a meaningful amount of assistance to those who need it the most without giving large amounts to those who are not poor, the program has to reduce rather rapidly the amount that individuals receive as their earned income increases. That means that high marginal tax rates on earned income are built into politically feasible transfer programs designed to reduce poverty. An individual who is receiving assistance from several programs (not uncommon), such as aid for families with dependent children (AFDC), food stamps, and Medicaid, can find the value of this assistance reduced from 70 to 90 percent for every additional dollar earned.[2] Obviously, the motivation to work is reduced when earning an additional dollar results in an increase in take-home income of only 10 to 30 cents, which then may be subject to more conventional taxation. Not surprisingly, as public welfare expenditures have increased, so has the percentage of the heads of poor households who are not employed. In 1959, for example, 30.5 percent of poor households were headed by an individual who did not

[2]See James Gwartney and Richard Stroup, "Transfers, Equality, and the Limits of Public Policy," *Cato Journal* 6, no. 1 (Spring/Summer 1986): 111–37.

work during the entire year; by 1987 this proportion had increased to 45 percent.[3]

Many factors are no doubt responsible for the decrease in work effort on the part of the poor, and it would be misleading to put all of the blame on transfer payments. Efforts have been made to isolate the transfer-payment effect on the work effort of the poor. Based on a number of studies concerned with the labor supply effects of social security, disability insurance, and AFDC, economists Sheldon Danziger, Robert Haveman, and Robert Plotnick estimated that, in the absence of transfer payments, the poor would have increased the number of hours they worked by 4.8 percent during the 1970s.[4] Although that may seem a relatively small increase (and some studies do indicate larger effects), this reduction in work effort translates into a reduction in earning equal to approximately 23 percent of the value of the transfers to the nonelderly poor in 1978.[5] In other words, after accounting for decreased work effort, the poor gained only 77 cents for every dollar they received from government. In a subsequent study, Plotnick put this net gain at only 29 to 42 cents.[6] Welfare payments provide an opportunity to substitute publicly provided income for privately earned income, and welfare recipients have taken advantage of this opportunity to a significant degree. The long-run consequences of this substitution are more adverse to the recipients' well-being than are the short-run consequences, given the importance of work experience in improving job skills and future earning potential.

Another critical feature of any poverty program is that if it is effective in helping the poor, it lowers the cost of being poor. Just as with a high marginal income tax on the poor, a reduction in the cost of being poor reduces the incentive for the poor to do things that overcome poverty and to avoid doing those things (such as

[3]These figures are reported in Gwartney and Stroup and in Bureau of the Census, *Statistical Abstract of the United States: 1990* (Washington: Government Printing Office, 1990), Table 750 (p. 462).

[4]See Sheldon Danziger, Robert Haveman, and Robert Plotnick, "How Income Transfer Programs Affect Work, Saving, and the Income Distribution: A Critical Analysis," *Journal of Economic Literature* 19 (September 1981): 975–1028.

[5]See ibid.

[6]See Robert Plotnick, "The Redistributive Impact of Cash Transfers," *Public Finance Quarterly* 12 (January 1984): 27–50.

dropping out of school, becoming an unwed mother, or developing a drug habit) that increase the probability of becoming or remaining poor (see the discussion above on the effect of transfer payments on an individual's decision to work).

Another perverse feature is that the availability of welfare to mothers with dependent children encourages women to worry less about establishing or maintaining a two-parent household with the father of their children. Similarly, welfare may reduce the sense of responsibility that fathers would otherwise feel for their children, thereby increasing the number of female-headed households— households that have a high incidence of poverty. Again, many factors interact in complex ways to influence the decisions that lead to female-headed households, but several studies have found positive relationships between welfare payments and the number of such households. Research indicates, for example, that a $100 increase in the maximum AFDC benefit per month (in 1975 dollars) for a family of four increases the number of female-headed households by 15 percent.[7] Data from an income-maintenance experiment in Seattle and Denver indicate that experimental families (those receiving income maintenance) experienced rates of marital breakup 50 percent higher than did families in the control group.[8]

Another and related feature is that the availability of welfare payments causes an increase in the number of children born out of wedlock. Once more at issue is a phenomenon that is influenced by a complex set of social and economic factors. According to a 1988 survey article on poverty in the United States, "no study has been able to establish a clear relationship between this trend [in out-of-wedlock childbearing] and the welfare system."[9] However, in a study based on a sample of unwed pregnant teenagers, it was concluded—after statistically controlling for such factors as age, religion, school enrollment, and ethnic origin—that those eligible for public assistance were significantly more likely to have babies

[7]The research is reported in Isabel V. Sawhill, "Poverty in the U.S.: Why Is It So Persistent?" *Journal of Economic Literature* 26 (September 1988): 1073–119. It should be pointed out that Sawhill also reported on other studies that suggest smaller effects.

[8]See Sawhill.

[9]See Sawhill, p. 1105.

out of wedlock.[10] It is undeniable that welfare payments lower the cost of having children out of wedlock—and that lowering the cost of any activity tends to increase its incidence.

To the extent that welfare does increase the incidence of single-parent households and unwed teenage mothers, it not only increases the number who currently depend on government transfers but also fosters an environment that tends to perpetuate that dependency. Few observers would disagree that those who are born out of wedlock or into broken homes, particularly broken homes that depend on welfare, are less likely than others to develop the skills and attitudes conducive to becoming productive and self-sufficient adults.[11] Again, it is recognized that many factors other than welfare contribute to the prospects of those who are born into homes receiving welfare. And no one would deny that, given the unfortunate circumstances into which many poor children are born, the income provided by public welfare can improve the prospects of such children. But it would also be naive to deny that the availability of public welfare increases, at least to some extent, the prevalence of these unfortunate circumstances and the number of children who are born into them.

With any program to help the poor, whether public or private, there exists the tendency to encourage poverty by reducing the cost of behaving in ways that increase the likelihood of poverty. But there are reasons for believing that such problems are less troublesome in the case of private giving to the poor than in the case of public giving. One reason to expect that private charities are more effective than public transfers at reducing recipient dependency is competition. A private charity has to acquire its budget through voluntary donations in competition with other private charities. And although few donors take the trouble to monitor the effectiveness of the private charity to which they contribute, some

[10]See Victor R. Fuchs, *How We Live: An Economic Perspective on Americans from Birth to Death* (Cambridge, Mass.: Harvard University Press, 1983), pp. 105–06.

[11]For example, evidence indicates that children born out of wedlock are neglected and abused with higher probability than normal. See Fuchs, p. 28. There is also a study that concludes that the people most likely to become AFDC recipients are those whose mothers were AFDC recipients. This study is reported in Morley D. Glicken, "Transgenerational Welfare Dependency," *Journal of Contemporary Studies* 4 (Summer 1981): 31–41.

do. A private charity has to be concerned that poor performance will be publicized and, as a consequence, its donors will redirect their generosity. Certainly a public welfare agency has less reason to be concerned than a private charity that its budget will be threatened by performance that is poor relative to that of a competing agency.[12]

It is also important to recognize that private charity leads to more competition on the recipient side of the market than does public charity. This competition reduces the likelihood that a recipient can exploit the availability of transfers by becoming dependent on them rather than making an effort to become self-sufficient. A private charity sees advantages in making use of its resources to provide aid to those who will use the aid productively. Private charities certainly have the ability and the motivation to refuse aid to those who appear to be taking unproductive advantage of it.

In the case of public welfare, considerations of due process and equal protection procedures result in eligibility requirements that sort people out in terms of broad categories rather than in accordance with fine and often subjective distinctions. Private agencies have more latitude than public agencies to make such subjective judgments and act on them in the effort to make the age-old distinction between the deserving and undeserving poor.

It should also be pointed out that the receipt of private charity is likely to make a recipient more deserving than is the receipt of public charity. A recipient can be expected to feel differently about the receipt of a private transfer provided voluntarily than about a public transfer required by law. With a private donation the recipient is more likely to experience a sense of gratitude for the help provided and a sense of obligation to those who provided it. Such gratitude and obligation are certainly important factors in motivating an individual to make productive, and therefore temporary, use of the help provided. Assistance from public agencies is more likely to be provided and received impersonally, and viewed as a

---

[12]The graft and corruption at the Department of Housing and Urban Development (HUD) and the agency's pitiful performance in carrying out its mission of providing housing for the poor have not resulted in a reduction in the huge HUD budget. Can anyone doubt that if a private charitable organization such as Goodwill Industries experienced a scandal as serious as that at HUD, its ability to raise money would be severely eroded?

right by the recipient with no sense of gratitude or obligation to those who provide it. The likely result is less reluctance to take advantage of public assistance by becoming reliant on it.[13]

Although we believe that private aid is more likely to be effective in motivating recipients to help themselves, we have no evidence as to how significant the difference is. The unfortunate fact is that any attempt to help the poor, whether public or private, prompts responses on the part of the poor that reduce the effectiveness of that help.

The Response of Donors

We now turn our attention to those who pay for transfers, both as taxpayers and as contributors to private charities. Donors respond to increases in government assistance to the poor, and their responses, like those of the recipients, erode the effectiveness of that assistance.

Public transfers to those with lower incomes obviously require taxes on those with higher incomes, and such taxes discourage productive activities. When higher income workers reduce their saving and productive effort, it not only reduces their incomes but also—by reducing the general productivity of the economy— reduces incomes in general, including those of the poor. This general reduction in productivity serves to offset somewhat the benefits the poor derive from the public transfers they receive.

It has been argued that the disincentive effect from taxation on the nonpoor is small and therefore not a significant consideration.[14] Casual observation may suggest, for example, that workers do not cut back the hours they work each week in response to a tax increase, and indeed most workers would find it difficult to cut back even if they wanted to. But some workers do have a choice in how many hours they work per week or how long a vacation they take, and almost all workers have some control over when

[13]For more on this point, see Dwight R. Lee and Richard B. McKenzie, "Second Thoughts on the Public-Good Justification for Government Poverty Programs," *Journal of Legal Studies* 19 (January 1990): 189–202.

[14]An economist who specializes in poverty issues has stated that "it should be stressed that while income transfer programs create disincentives to work and save, the magnitude of these disincentives is relatively small. They pose no threat to the overall efficiency of the economy." See Sheldon Danziger, "Poverty and Inequality under Reaganomics," *Journal of Contemporary Studies* 5 (Summer 1982): 17–30.

they enter the workforce, when they retire, how hard they apply themselves on the job, how diligently they prepare for promotions, and whether they take a second job. And the evidence shows clearly that work effort does decline in response to higher taxes on income.

Furthermore, even if the negative response in work effort to a tax increase is small, it does not follow that the effect of this reduction on government attempts to transfer income to the poor will be small. Economists Edgar Browning and William Johnson have considered the cost to donor taxpayers of transferring an additional dollar to those who are poor. Assuming that work effort will decline by 3.1 percent in response to a 10 percent reduction in after-tax income, a decline that seems reasonable given the results of empirical studies, Browning and Johnson estimated that it costs taxpayers $9.51 to transfer an additional $1 to the poor.[15] When they considered the further negative effect of taxation and transfers on savings in the economy, they concluded that it is possible that transferring an additional dollar to the poor leaves everyone worse off, including the poor.

It should be emphasized that the Browning and Johnson results apply only to the effect of transferring an additional dollar to the poor, not to the effect of transferring income to the poor on average. In other words, transferring one more dollar to the poor could result in the poor being worse off after accounting for the decline in overall economic efficiency, even though transfers to the poor up to that point increased the net income of the poor. It is clear, however, that the labor and saving response of the nonpoor (as well as the poor) to transfers to the poor can have a significant effect on the net benefit the poor receive from the transfers.

---

[15]See Edgar K. Browning and William R. Johnson, "The Trade-Off between Equality and Efficiency," *Journal of Political Economy* 92 (April 1984): 175–203; and Edgar K. Browning and William R. Johnson, "The Cost of Reducing Inequality," *Cato Journal* 6 (Spring/Summer 1986): 85–109. The Browning and Johnson estimate of the cost of transferring an additional dollar to the poor is based on a transfer scheme similar to that of the negative income tax proposals recommended by economists as being more efficient than current transfer programs. It is also based entirely on the loss resulting from the decline in work effort resulting from the taxes needed to finance the transfers, and it does not consider any costs associated with the administration of welfare programs.

The nonpoor respond to government transfers to the poor not only as workers and savers but also as contributors to private charities that help the poor. It is reasonable to expect that the amount contributed to private charities will decrease with increases in government spending supposedly designated for the purpose of providing assistance to the poor. And the evidence supports this expectation. Economists Burt Abrams and Mark Schmitz, using data from the years 1948–72, found that, for every dollar increase in government's welfare expenditures, contributions to private charities were reduced by 28 cents.[16] Using more recent data and a different empirical approach, they performed another study of the connection between public welfare expenditures and private charitable contributions and found that every dollar of public welfare crowded out 30 cents of private charity.[17]

The evidence from these crowding-out studies likely underestimates the negative impact of public transfers to the poor on private transfers to the poor. It is important to recognize that the studies by Abrams and Schmitz follow the Internal Revenue Service in defining private charity. The problem with this approach is that U.S. tax law allows contributions to qualify as tax-deductible charitable contributions even though they may have little if anything to do with helping the poor. When the composition of these contributions is examined, it is found that as public transfers began increasing in the 1930s, private giving shifted significantly away from helping the poor and went increasingly toward the support of religious organizations, education, health, and the arts. In a study of the effect of public transfer programs on the composition of private giving, economist Russell Roberts concluded, "The huge growth in public transfer in the 1930s crowded out private antipoverty efforts and fundamentally changed the nature of private charity."[18]

---

[16]See Burt Abrams and Mark Schmitz, "The 'Crowding-out' Effect of Government Transfers on Private Charitable Contributions," *Public Choice* 33, no. 1 (1978): 28–40.

[17]See Burt Abrams and Mark Schmitz, "The 'Crowding-out' Effect of Government Transfers on Private Charitable Contributions: Cross-Sectional Evidence," *National Tax Journal* 37, no. 4 (December 1984): 563–68.

[18]See Russell D. Roberts, "A Positive Model of Private Charity and Public Transfers," *Journal of Political Economy* 92 (February 1984): 147.

To use an analogy from Adam Smith, people are not like pieces on a chessboard that do only what some controlling authority wants them to do. People respond to attempts to influence their behavior in ways that often frustrate those attempts.

The Politics of Helping the Poor

In addition to the problem discussed above, there are reasons for believing that the democratic political process is severely limited in its ability to transfer wealth to the poor. Indeed, when all of the effects of government attempts to make transfers in the name of helping the poor are considered, it is very likely that government transfers have reduced rather than increased the wealth of the poor.

To examine the problem government faces in any attempt to transfer income to the poor, we now reconsider how government outcomes are determined. It is commonly assumed that such outcomes are determined in a fundamentally different way than market outcomes. The problem of poverty illustrates this assumed difference. Poverty is seen to result from a market process that is driven by competition between self-seeking individuals who are unconcerned with the impact of their actions on such broad social considerations as the distribution of income. There is little doubt that this perception of the market process is an accurate one. When competing for a better job, for example, how many people concern themselves with whether their actions will make the income distribution more unequal? The aggregate effect of market competition is a distribution of income that is unequal, with those who possess productive skills receiving more than those without such skills. It is this distribution of income that is seen to justify government actions designed to assist those whom the market has left behind. This justification typically comes with the implicit assumption that the political process, as opposed to the market process, is motivated by people's desire to achieve broad social objectives such as reducing income inequality. It is assumed that, in their political roles, people want to help the poor, and that it is a straightforward political exercise to take income from the nonpoor and make it available to the poor.

But what is the basis for assuming that people have a different set of motivations when making political decisions than when making market decisions? There is no evidence of which we are aware that a moral metamorphosis of any type occurs when people move from market activity to political activity. Does anyone believe, for example, that unionized automobile workers are more concerned with equity in the overall distribution of income when taking political action in support of automobile import restrictions that will increase their incomes than when negotiating privately with their employers for higher incomes? If one wants to make a realistic assessment of how effectively government could improve upon the market in solving social problems, it is self-defeating to bias the conclusion by assuming that people are intent on promoting their own objectives when making market decisions and intent on promoting social objectives when making political decisions.

The far more plausible assumption is that people are no less self-regarding in one setting than in another. No matter where ordinary people find themselves, they can usually be depended on to do the best they can to advance their own interests. And in the political arena, no less than in the marketplace, that means that people will find themselves in competition with one another. In other words, political outcomes are determined in the same general way as are market outcomes. The political process, just as the market process, is driven by competition between individuals who are far more interested in promoting their private objectives than they are in promoting broad social objectives. The outcomes of the political process are not the result of a consensus on shared objectives, but rather they emerge as the largely unintended consequences of the competitive political interaction among those with many different, and often conflicting, objectives.

Once it is accepted that the political process is one based on competition, the idea that government can be relied upon to redistribute income from the nonpoor to the poor is called immediately into question. If people are poor because they do not have the skills necessary to succeed in market competition, is there any basis for believing that they have the skills necessary to succeed in political competition? Is there any evidence that the skills required in political competition are different from those required in market competition or, if they are different, that political skills are more evenly distributed over the population than market skills? If not, then there is no reason for believing that increasing the share of the national income allocated through political competition will help

118

the poor by reducing income inequality. There is no reason that we can think of for believing that any differences that may exist between market skills and political skills are such that market competition will generate either more or less inequality than political competition. But we have never heard anyone who recommends government programs to help the poor acknowledge the importance of such differences to the success of such programs, much less argue that the differences exist and favor political competition over market competition as a means for helping the poor.

There are important differences, of course, between political competition and market competition. The view that individuals compete on the basis of self-interest when making political decisions just as they do when making market decisions does not imply that they will behave the same in one setting as in the other. Political rules differ from market rules, and each set of rules assigns different costs and benefits to similar activities. If, relative to market rules, political rules lower the costs or increase the benefits of an activity, then self-interest will dictate that people engage in that activity to a greater extent as political actors than as market actors. And in some important ways, political rules do make it less costly for individuals to act on their sense of generosity than do market rules. At the same time, it is also true that there are important ways in which political rules make it possible for special-interest groups to exploit political generosity for their private advantage and in doing so undermine any good that might have resulted from the generosity.

Most people do get a sense of satisfaction from helping others and are willing to do so, at least up to some point, even at a personal cost to themselves. Such generosity is entirely consistent with the pursuit of self-interest broadly defined. But self-interest dictates that the degree to which one behaves generously depends on the cost. But it is less costly to act in response to one's sense of generosity in a political setting than in a market setting (see chapter 7).

Therefore, if an individual derives a sense of satisfaction from expressing generosity at the polls, he will do so with little regard for the potential cost of that generosity. That contrasts sharply with the generosity that is expressed in private giving. The decision to make a $50 contribution to a private charity is decisive; it determines with certainty how much will be paid, and therefore it costs the

119

donor $50. This cost cannot be ignored and serves to restrain private generosity. Predictably, people will express more generosity through their political behavior than through their market behavior.

It takes more than the costless expression of generosity at the polls, however, to ensure benefits for the poor. Transfer programs have to be properly designed to minimize the disincentive effects, and even well-designed programs have to be properly implemented if they are to be effective. But it is extraordinarily difficult to properly design and effectively implement government poverty programs. Even if everyone were more committed to increasing the well-being of the poor than to increasing his own well-being, political attempts to help the poor would still face a range of problems (as discussed above). And few people are more committed to helping the poor than they are to helping themselves. The political power necessary to transfer income to the poor is power that can be used to transfer income to the nonpoor, and the nonpoor generally are more adept than the poor at using political power. Political power has to be coupled with public scrutiny if it is to effectively promote public purposes such as reducing poverty.

As opposed to the act of voting in favor of a poverty program, however, the act of monitoring the effectiveness of the program once it receives political approval is personally costly. How many people, after voting to assist the poor, go to the considerable personal expense of becoming politically involved in working for more efficient poverty programs? Not many. With few if any exceptions, those who support poverty programs at the polls give the problem of poverty little more thought, except to occasionally lament the news reports of continued poverty and to feel good about the compassion they expressed at the polls. That does not mean that no one will go to the expense of becoming actively involved politically. Many will. But when people become politically involved, it is typically to lobby for, and influence the structure of, government programs that provide them with significant private benefits, not to increase government efficiency in promoting broad social objectives such as poverty reduction. Again, that is not to say that people never take political action to improve public policy for the general betterment of society. Obviously they do. But working for improved public policy is the same as contributing to a public good, such as national defense,[19] and the rationale for having government force people to contribute to such goods is that individuals have little motivation to do so voluntarily. If people could be depended on to become involved politically for the purpose of improving public policy with the same dedication that they do to obtain special advantages for themselves, there would be little need for government in the first place.

It is useful to consider the interests of those most likely to be politically involved in determining the structure and performance of government poverty programs. One group with a dominant interest in such programs consists of those whose employment is tied to the programs. Included in this group are those employed directly by government welfare agencies or as private contractors and academic researchers to assist and advise the agencies. As with most people, poverty professionals have an overriding interest in their incomes and job security and can be expected to favor the continuation and expansion of funding for poverty programs independently of the benefits the poor receive from them. Typically, those who are employed directly or indirectly by poverty agencies are better educated and more politically informed and active than the average citizen and are well organized through employee and professional associations. In addition, they have credibility as experts on the problems of poverty. Consequently, poverty professionals not only have a vested interest in the funding and implementation of poverty programs but also have the political clout to influence policy in accordance with that interest.

Another group with a strong private interest in poverty programs consists of those who supply products that it is believed the poor should have but cannot be depended on to buy, even if they have sufficient income. Of the means-tested income transfers (provided only to recipients with sufficiently low incomes) in 1984, only 30 percent were in the form of cash payments.[20] The remaining aid takes the form of such items as food, medical attention, housing, counseling, and educational benefits. One can be sure that such politically effective interest groups as the agricultural lobby, the

---

[19]See Gordon Tullock, "Public Policy as a Public Good," *Journal of Political Economy* 79 (July/August 1971): 913–18.

[20]See Sawhill, Table 4 (p. 1098).

American Medical Association (AMA), and construction and educational associations have significant influence on decisions regarding the composition of welfare spending. Is anyone really surprised that the incomes of doctors were increased by programs, such as Medicaid, that provide the poor with medical care, or that the AMA had significant influence on the design of the Medicaid program?

The poor, of course, are interested in government welfare programs and favor programs that are as effective as possible. However, they cannot be expected to have much influence on the details of government antipoverty efforts. It has to be recognized that most of those who are officially counted as poor at any one time (those whose incomes are below the official poverty line) do not think of themselves as poor and have little interest in poverty programs. Many people fall temporarily below the poverty line at one time or another, even those such as medical students whose lifetime incomes are high. Relatively few people remain below the poverty line for long.[21] Therefore, when talking about the poor who can be expected to have an overriding interest in poverty programs, we are talking about the small proportion that is chronically poor. They are people, however, who typically have special problems that limit severely their ability to pursue objectives effectively through either private or political activity. If the poor had the skills and ability to be effective in competing for political influence, it is unlikely that they would be poor in the first place. The plight of the poor is certainly used, and even exaggerated on occasion, by politically influential groups with a vested interest in expanding government poverty programs. But the poor themselves have little influence on the design of those programs or on how effectively their interests are served by them.

As government welfare recipients, the poor depend on their interests corresponding with the interests of those who administer and supply government welfare programs. In some ways these interests do correspond. Both welfare recipients and poverty professionals have an interest in maintaining and expanding social

[21]For example, a recent study indicates that 24.4 percent of the population was officially considered poor during at least one year over the period 1969–78. But only 2.6 percent of the population was below the poverty line in eight out of those ten years. See Greg Duncan, *Years of Poverty, Years of Plenty* (Ann Arbor: University of Michigan Press, 1984). These figures are also cited in Sawhill, p. 1080.

welfare budgets. But the professionals realize benefits from expanding their budgets that are independent of whether that expansion serves the interests of the poor. Regardless of how effectively the budget of a government agency is spent, those who work for that agency are likely to receive more promotions, perquisites, prestige, power, and job security if the agency is expanding rather than contracting. Accordingly, professionals in transfer agencies are interested in structuring their programs so that they have as much political appeal as possible, even if that requires reducing the programs' effectiveness in helping the poor.

Increasing a welfare program's political support requires making sure that politically influential groups benefit from the program's expansion. One way of doing that is to shift the mix of the benefits going to the poor toward in-kind rather than cash benefits. When a government antipoverty effort is relatively small, one might expect that there will be heavy reliance on cash transfers, certainly the easiest and most effective means of helping people in poverty. As opposed to cash transfers, however, transfers of particular products will benefit the highly organized interest groups that produce such products. A transfer agency proposing to increase its budget by expanding the amount of industry X's product transferred to the poor can count on the political support of industry X. That suggests that as government welfare spending increases, the increase will be heavily weighted in favor of in-kind transfers. The evidence leaves no doubt that that is the case. In 1960, U.S. government expenditures on means-tested programs were $16 billion, with $13 billion (over 81 percent of the total) taking the form of cash transfers and the rest being $3 billion worth of in-kind transfers. In 1984, government expenditures on means-tested programs were $100 billion, with $30 billion (30 percent of the total) taking the form of cash and $70 billion being in in-kind transfers. In other words, between 1960 and 1984, cash transfers to the poor increased 130 percent while in-kind benefits increased over 2,233 percent.[22]

It is also in the interest of the transfer establishment to expand public generosity to include new recipients. Once a transfer program is in place to help the poor, other purportedly deserving,

---

[22]See Sawhill, Table 4 (p. 1098).

though not necessarily poor, groups will see benefit in mobilizing political support for expanding the program to include them. The effectiveness of such interest-group activity generally increases with time.[23] Therefore, the longer a transfer program has been in existence, the greater the political pressure to expand the funding of the program—and to do so in ways that broaden the number who benefit from it.[24]

After relatively modest beginnings in the mid-1960s, the funding for a number of welfare programs escalated rapidly.[25] Medicaid, which pays for the medical care of the poor, grew to become a $34.2 billion program in 1989, from an initial program of $500 million in 1965. The food stamp program cost $13.5 billion in 1986 compared to $40 million in 1965. The AFDC budget was $17.8 billion in 1986, compared with $1.7 billion in 1965 (AFDC was established in the 1930s). Over the same interval the annual cost of housing assistance for the poor increased to $13.3 billion from $300 million.

It is probably true that the poor benefited from the political pressures that generated this increased spending on these means-tested programs. It should be kept in mind, however, that the poor do not receive nearly as much benefit from the increased spending on these programs as the dollar amounts would indicate. Most of the means-tested aid now takes the form of in-kind transfers, and the value that the poor place on such aid is less than the cost of providing it for at least two reasons. First, if the poor were given the cash equivalent of the in-kind aid they received, they would purchase that same bundle of goods only if they valued the bundle of in-kind goods at their market price. The justification for giving in-kind aid rather than cash is that the poor would not purchase that

[23]For an extended argument supporting the view that special-interest groups become more politically influential over time and a discussion of the wide-ranging implications of this increasing influence, see Mancur Olson, Jr., *The Rise and Decline of Nations* (New Haven: Yale University Press, 1982).

[24]There are obvious limits on the growth of special-interest programs. If a program favored by one interest group expands, to some extent it does so at the expense of a program favored by another politically influential group. But this conflict can be moderated by pushing back the political budget constraint by imposing more cost on the unorganized public. And that is exactly what politicians are under constant pressure to do.

[25]These figures are from Danziger, Haveman, and Plotnick, Table 1; and Bureau of the Census, *Abstract of the United States: 1990*, Table 141 (p. 95).

same bundle of goods. But that justification acknowledges that the value the poor receive from the in-kind aid is less than its market value. Second, whether government is contracting for military hardware from a defense contractor or medical care from the medical industry, experience suggests that the suppliers overcharge for the goods and services provided.[26] In the case of in-kind transfers to the poor, much of the expenditure represents benefits to suppliers rather than benefits to the poor.

Leakage between the expenditures by government welfare programs and the benefits received by the poor is present to a significant degree even in that portion of the aid that takes the form of cash. In 1983, for example, $31 billion was spent on means-tested cash assistance programs. If that entire amount had been delivered effectively to the poor, the poverty gap (the amount of money it would take to raise all of the poor up to the official poverty line), which before cash transfers was $63 billion in 1983, would have been reduced to $32 billion. In fact, only $16 billion of the $31 billion in cash actually reached the poor, and the poverty gap after the receipt of all cash transfers in 1983 declined only to $47 billion.[27] But even with the leakages to the poor taken into consideration, it is still reasonable to conclude that some benefits from means-tested programs do trickle down to the poor.

It does not follow, however, that on balance the poor are beneficiaries of public assistance programs and the political influence that leads to the programs' expansion. That influence transforms government transfer activities aimed primarily at the poor into

[26]Before 1983, for example, hospitals had a strong incentive to overcharge for Medicare patients because Medicare reimbursed hospitals for whatever they charged within lenient limits. After 1983 Medicare set prices that it would pay for medical procedures. Doctors and hospitals responded to this cost-containment measure by performing more and costlier procedures on Medicare patients. See Julie Kosterlitz, "Cut with Care," *National Journal*, December 10, 1988, pp. 3116–20.

[27]See Sawhill, p. 1101. There are reasons for the gap between the amount spent and the reduction in the poverty gap other than excessive administrative expenses. Even means-tested programs often extend eligibility to those who have pre-transfer incomes above the poverty line, with the cut-off for some programs being set as high as 185 percent above the poverty line. See Domestic Policy Council Low Income Opportunity Group, *Up from Dependency: A New National Public Assistance Strategy* (Washington; Government Printing Office, December 1986), p. 18. When in-kind transfers are included, over 50 percent of all people who receive welfare have pre-welfare incomes above the poverty line. Ibid., p. 36.

programs that extend benefits to those who are not poor. Even if the poor continue to receive the same level of benefits that they would have received without the expansion of benefits to the non-poor, the poor can still be worse off by virtue of the fact that they pay for at least part of this expansion through their own taxes. Also, once the nonpoor begin competing for the transfers that had initially been justified to help the poor, the poor may find that they are receiving less than they otherwise would. The nonpoor already have outcompeted the poor in the private sector, and there is little reason to doubt that they will do the same in the public sector. It should come as no surprise that soon after Medicaid was established to publicly fund medical care for the poor, Medicare was enacted to publicly fund medical care for those over the age of 65 no matter what their incomes. And while annual Medicaid expenditures increased to $34.2 billion by 1989, annual Medicare expenditures increased to $86.7 billion, despite the fact that the number of people officially designated as poor is greater than the number of people over 65.[28] Furthermore, those over 65 have nearly twice the net worth on average as the entire population.[29]

Of total social welfare expenditures, those that are means-tested make up only about 21 percent. In 1984, in addition to government expenditures of $100 billion on means-tested programs, $375 billion was spent on non-means-tested programs such as Medicare, old-age, social security, railroad retirement, unemployment insurance, workers' compensation, government employment pensions, and veterans' pensions and compensations. Some of these non-means-tested transfers, of course, went to those who were poor, but most of them did not. And one can be sure that those who benefit from

[28]The expenditure figures for Medicaid and Medicare come from Bureau of the Census, *Statistical Abstract of the United States: 1990*, Table 141 (p. 95). In 1988 there were 30.4 million Americans aged 65 or older. Ibid., Table 13 (p. 13). That compares with 31.9 million people officially designated as poor in 1988. Ibid., Table 743 (p. 458).

[29]In 1984 the median net worth of households headed by those aged 65 or older was $60,266, as compared to a median net worth of $32,667 for all households. Bureau of the Census, *Statistical Abstract of the United States: 1988* (Washington: Government Printing Office, 1988), Table 727 (p. 440). For a detailed discussion of how Medicare discriminates against the poor, see John C. Goodman and Gerald L. Musgrave, *Patient Power: Solving America's Health Care Crisis* (Washington: Cato Institute, 1992), pp. 425–27.

these non-means-tested programs are quite capable of competing for political influence against those who benefit from the means-tested programs. Indeed, expenditures on the non-means-tested programs increased by 42 percent between 1975 and 1984, while expenditures on means-tested programs increased by 19 percent.[30]

So far, we have been discussing programs, whether means-tested or not, that can plausibly be justified as an appropriate means of helping those who have lost income because of such things as unemployment, disability, retirement, or the loss of the primary breadwinner. Many government transfers, however, have nothing to do with helping those who are poor or who are at risk of becoming poor. But all such transfer programs are supported by politically influential constituencies that have both the ability and motivation to depict the goals and recipients of the programs as being worthy of public assistance. And the special-interest pressure to fund such programs, when accompanied by the rhetoric of noble public objectives, typically is reinforced by support at the polls. The individual voter, when deciding whether to vote for or against a deserving program to benefit the nonpoor, attaches no greater personal cost to a favorable vote than he does when voting in favor of helping the poor. In both cases his vote is so unlikely to be decisive that the cost of voting on the side of compassion and virtue is effectively zero. If people who feel good about making a statement in favor of assisting the poor at the polls feel just as good about making a statement in favor of other noble objectives as well, the result can be unfortunate for the poor. Such generalized generosity makes it that much easier for a wide variety of special-interest coalitions to outcompete the poor for political influence and public beneficence.

It is easy to find virtue, for example, in providing financial assistance to capable students who otherwise would not be able to attend college. To provide such assistance, the federal government established a subsidized student loan program in 1957, limiting eligibility to students from low-income families. Over time, however, associations representing higher education and students were able to mobilize increasing political pressure in favor of expanding eligibility for student loan subsidies. The same pressure was also applied to eligibility for Pell grants, which provide federal grants

[30]See Sawhill, Table 4 (p. 1098).

to college students through their schools. In 1978 Congress responded to this pressure by making subsidized student loans and Pell grants available to students from high-income families as well as to those from low-income families.[31] Guaranteed student loans went from a $1.5 billion program in 1977 to a $7.8 billion program in 1981, and the Pell grant program went from $1.5 billion to $2.5 billion over the same period.[32] The purpose here is not to evaluate the desirability of these programs, but to note that they changed from programs providing assistance primarily to poor students to programs providing assistance primarily to nonpoor students.

In the competition for government assistance, the agricultural lobby has been able to take advantage of the public's image of the small family farm as a source of American strength and virtue. Although the public supports farm income stabilization programs, which cost the taxpayers $29.6 billion in their peak year of 1986, few individuals seem to be aware that most of the benefits from these programs go to large agribusiness operations, not to small family farms.[33] And even if agricultural programs allocated benefits more evenly among farms, they would be transferring money from those with less wealth to those with more. In 1985, for example, the net worth of the average U.S. farm was $299,999, which compares with a 1984 median household net worth in the United States of $32,667.[34] Furthermore, agricultural programs have done nothing to slow the reduction in the number of small family farms and the shift toward large farm operations, and they have likely encouraged this trend. Because most such programs pay more to farmers who

[31]Congress passed Public Law 95566, which the president signed into law on November 1, 1978.

[32]The budget figures were compiled from Bureau of the Census, *Statistical Abstract of the United States: 1984* (Washington: Government Printing Office, 1984), p. 166.

[33]In 1986, government payments of $11.8 billion were distributed among farms of different sizes (as discussed in chapter 6). The $29.6 billion figure cited here includes government loans to farmers who put up their crops for collateral. Essentially, these loans are sales of crops to the government at above-market prices and are distributed among farms in much the same way as direct payments. For a good discussion of agricultural price support programs, see James Bovard, *The Farm Fiasco* (San Francisco: ICS Press, 1989).

[34]Compiled from Bureau of the Census, *Statistical Abstract of the United States: 1988*, pp. 441, 613.

128

produce more, they have created incentives for larger but fewer farms. In 1940, for example, there were 6.1 million farms in the United States, with an average of 173 acres per farm;[35] by 1989 there were only 2.2 million farms, with an average of 456 acres per farm.[36]

From the perspective of either economic efficiency or equity, agricultural transfer programs are unequivocal failures. But they are a huge success in the arena of special-interest politics and provide another example of the nonpoor outcompeting the poor for government assistance. Furthermore, because of government agricultural programs, the poor pay inflated prices for much of their food—and also higher taxes to finance the programs.

There are many government programs that transfer enormous amounts of wealth from the politically unorganized to the politically organized, but that do not show up in the government budget. For example, in response to pressure from domestic industries facing foreign competition, the federal government imposes import restrictions on a host of products. Although, these restrictions help the organized few who are protected, they increase the prices paid by all consumers and reduce the general efficiency of the economy. Import restrictions on sugar increase the total food bill of American consumers by a little over $3 billion per year, which works out to about $260,000 for each domestic sugar producer.[37] A 1980 study by the Federal Trade Commission estimated that import restrictions on textiles cost American consumers nearly $6 billion per year.[38] A 1983 study by economist Michael Munger estimated that the annual cost to consumers (in 1980 dollars) of import restrictions on a selected number of products came to $45.8 billion.[39] That cost is

[35]Compiled from Bureau of the Census, *Statistical Abstract of the United States: 1965* (Washington: Government Printing Office, 1965), pp. 614, 620.

[36]From Bureau of the Census, *Statistical Abstract of the United States: 1990*, Table 1101 (p. 638). It should be pointed out that much of this increase in farm size resulted from economic considerations that had nothing to do with farm subsidies.

[37]See Ralph Ives and John Hurley, *United States Sugar Policy and Analysis* (Washington: Department of Commerce, 1988).

[38]See Morris E. Morkre and David G. Tarr, *Effects of Restriction on United States Imports: Case Studies and Theory* (Washington: Federal Trade Commission, 1980), p. 197.

[39]See Michael C. Munger, "The Costs of Protectionism: Estimates of the Hidden Tax of Trade Restraints," Working Paper no. 80 (St. Louis: Center for the Study of American Business, Washington University, July 1983).

certainly higher today because trade restrictions increased during the 1980s. The poor, as consumers, are harmed by these and a host of other import restrictions. And because such a large percentage of the income of the poor goes for food and clothing—products whose prices are artificially increased by import restrictions (as well as by other government programs)—the poor are harmed more by these restrictions than are the nonpoor.

It can be argued that import restrictions protect domestic jobs and thereby increase opportunities for the poor. The problem with this argument is that few if any of the poor are members of the unionized industries that are most likely to have the political influence to obtain protection against foreign competition. Also, saving some domestic jobs through the use of import restrictions results in the elimination of other jobs. And often it is lower income workers whose jobs are eliminated. That is what happened after import restrictions were imposed on steel in September 1984. The restrictions reduced steel imports from approximately 26 percent of the U.S. market in 1984 to about 22 percent in 1986.[40] They also achieved their objective of saving jobs in the domestic steel industry. It is estimated that 14,100 jobs were saved in basic steel production and another 2,800 more jobs were saved in firms supplying the steel industry. Unfortunately, the higher steel prices that resulted increased the costs of U.S. industries using steel, which reduced the demand for their products. And because of that reduced demand, it is estimated that 52,400 jobs were lost in those other industries. Taking the jobs saved into account, the restrictions resulted in a net loss of over 35,000 domestic jobs. Furthermore, the workers who lost their jobs earned on average about 40 percent less than the steel workers whose jobs were saved.[41] The import restrictions, therefore, did more than reduce the overall productivity of the U.S. economy. They also imposed losses on those with lower incomes and transferred wealth to those with higher incomes.

We could continue indefinitely with discussions of government programs that transfer wealth in response to special-interest competition. For our purpose, however, it is important to recognize that

[40]This account of the effects of steel import restrictions is based on Arthur T. Denzau, *How Import Restraints Reduce Employment*, Formal Publication no. 80 (St. Louis: Center for the Study of American Business, Washington University, June 1987).

[41]The average wage of steel workers in 1986 was over $30,000 a year. See Denzau.

all such programs have one thing in common: they all impose costs on the poor. That is true even of those programs that transfer wealth to the poor. The poor pay for all transfer programs, in most cases directly through higher taxes and prices, and in all cases indirectly through reduced economic efficiency. Despite these costs, the poor obviously are net beneficiaries of a special-interest program when it focuses the wealth transfer on them. But just as obviously, they are net losers from the many special-interest programs that transfer wealth primarily to the nonpoor.

Concluding Comments

The question mark in the title of this chapter reflects the suspicion that political attempts to help the poor directly have been failures. Assuming for the moment that this suspicion is correct, it has to be acknowledged that the failure is attributable partly to considerations that cannot be blamed on the political process. Any attempt to help the poor, whether public or private, is frustrated to some extent by the fact that success tends to undermine itself. To the degree that transfers help the poor, they also reduce the cost of being poor and therefore reduce the incentive to avoid poverty. Consequently, even if government programs are successful in transferring income from the nonpoor to the poor, they are not as successful in helping the poor as the size of the transfers might suggest.

But are government programs successful in transferring income to the poor? This chapter suggests that the answer to this question may be no—and if it is, we can remove the question mark from the chapter title. If the political process were under the direction of some benevolent force with the objective of protecting the poor against the harshness of market competition, then doubt about government's ability to transfer income to the poor would be misplaced. But no such unified force exists in government. The political arena is no less competitive than the marketplace, and the pattern of government outcomes emerges as the unintended by-products of the political interaction between competing interests. The rules are different, and so political competition leads to outcomes that differ in detail from those that emerge from market competition. There is no reason, however, to believe that those who do not do well in the marketplace will do any better on the field of political battle. Certainly our discussion in this chapter provides no reason for being optimistic that the poor are well served by attempting to increase the amount of national income that is distributed to them through government programs. But more evidence is needed to decide if, on balance, government transfer programs have helped or harmed the poor. Evidence bearing on this issue is considered in the next chapter.

9. Overcoming Failure with Hard-Hearted Compassion

To most people it seems obvious that government transfer programs are helping the poor. It is certainly possible to identify programs that do transfer income to them. Neither can there be any reasonable doubt that if these programs were eliminated, the poor who receive transfers from them would immediately become poorer. Nevertheless, as discussed in the previous chapter, it is not possible to judge accurately the success of government transfer programs at helping the poor by considering the short-run effects of particular programs without considering the long-run effects of government transfers in general.

Just as concentrating on particular short-run failures in the marketplace gives one a misleading impression of the long-run effects of the entire market process, so concentrating on particular short-run successes in the political arena gives one a misleading impression of the long-run effects of the entire political process. The political process that spawns a government program to transfer wealth to the poor is the same process that also transfers wealth to the nonpoor. There is reason, therefore, to doubt that the short-run effect of government transfers on income distribution does favor the poor, and, even if it does, to doubt that this effect is sufficient to overcome the long-run negative effects that government programs have on the amount of income available for distribution.

It is impossible to determine with complete confidence whether or not the poor are better off because of government transfers. But it is easy to show that the evidence commonly used to support the view that government transfers do help the poor not only fails to do so but also can be used to support the view that such transfers have harmed the poor. The best evidence on the effect of government transfers on the well-being of the poor comes from studies of changes in the after-tax/after-transfer distribution of income over time. These studies suggest strongly that the poor have not been well served by government.

The Actual versus the Counterfactual

There is no shortage of studies supporting the view that government transfer programs not only are helping the poor but are essential to their well-being.[1] The general approach of these studies is to compare the income of the poor (including their income from government transfers) with their income without these transfers. Having performed this calculation, it is possible to arrive at the percentage of people whose incomes are below the poverty line without government transfers but who have been lifted out of poverty by government transfers. The conclusion of such studies is that government transfers are responsible for preventing the poverty rate from being far higher than it is. A recent survey of these studies concludes, for example, that in 1985, transfer payments (including in-kind as well as cash transfers from both means-tested and non-means-tested programs) lifted out of poverty 41.6 percent of those who would otherwise have been poor.[2] It is all too easily concluded from such studies that government transfer programs have dramatically reduced the poverty rate and therefore clearly have helped the poor.

Such a conclusion is premature. The studies that compare post-transfer incomes with incomes that currently exist in the absence of transfers overstate the benefits the poor receive from government transfer for two important reasons.

The first reason involves the problem of determining what those who are receiving welfare payments would have received in the absence of those payments. If a meaningful assessment is to be made of the benefits the poor receive from welfare, one must take into consideration how the availability of welfare has affected the income the poor would have otherwise received from other sources.

---

[1]Many of these studies are discussed in Sheldon Danziger, Robert Haveman, and Robert Plotnick, "How Income Transfer Programs Affect Work, Saving, and the Income Distribution: A Critical Analysis," *Journal of Economic Literature* 19, no. 3 (September 1981): 1006–15.

[2]See Isabel V. Sawhill, "Poverty in the U.S.: Why Is It So Persistent?" *Journal of Economic Literature* 26 (September 1988): Table 5 (p. 1100).

In other words, one has to compare how much the poor are receiving with their welfare income against how much they would have received in a world in which government transfer payments did not exist.

The problem with making such a comparison is that no one can be sure what the income distribution would be in the counterfactual world of no government transfer payments. In response to this difficulty, the typical approach in the above-mentioned studies of the effectiveness of welfare in reducing poverty is simply to assume that government welfare programs have no effect on the nonwelfare income of the poor—that is, in comparison with a world in which welfare is unavailable, the poor are assumed to be better off by the full amount of the welfare payments they receive.[3] Obviously, that overstates the benefits the poor receive from welfare payments. As previously discussed, the response to the availability of transfer payments is a reduction in private charity and some substitution on the part of the poor of publicly provided income for privately earned income.

The second reason that the effectiveness of welfare programs is overstated is that they are considered separate from other government transfer programs. If government only transferred wealth from the nonpoor to the poor, then government transfers might indeed help the poor. But, as we have argued, a political process that makes it easy to transfer wealth to the poor with one program also makes it easy to transfer wealth to the nonpoor with another. The poor will come out net winners in some transfer programs, but they will be net losers on many more. Obviously, if one studies only the effects of the transfer programs for the poor and ignores the effects of those for the nonpoor, it will be possible to conclude that government transfer programs help the poor. But with the right assumptions, any conclusion is possible. And studies that assume that government transfers to the poor do not affect the income of the poor from other sources and that the poor are affected

[3]For example, after concluding that social welfare programs are significantly reducing poverty, Danziger, Haveman, and Plotnick acknowledged that the studies upon which they based their conclusion "adjust for neither the replacement of public by private transfers in the absence of the former, nor for the tendency of transfers to increase pre-transfer poverty by . . . reducing work effort . . . . " Danziger, Haveman, and Plotnick, p. 1018.

only by those government transfers they receive are sure to reach misleading conclusions.

With no way of knowing precisely how well the poor would have done in the counterfactual world without government transfers, it is impossible to reach a definitive conclusion on how well the poor have been served by these transfers. But to the extent that politics is a competitive process in which the poor face the same general disadvantages that they face in the market process, the aggregate effect of government transfers on the distribution of income is at best likely to be insignificant.

Studies that speak most directly to the effect of government transfers on the income distribution are those that examine changes in this distribution over time, after adjusting for the effects of taxes and transfers. One would presume, if government transfer programs were helping the poor, that the income distribution would have become more equal as government spending on poverty programs increased. The studies that have been done, however, indicate that the after-tax/after-transfer distribution of income has remained remarkably stable over the last four decades. One study by economists Morgan Reynolds and Eugene Smolensky, who adjusted the income distribution for tax payments and the value of in-kind as well as government cash transfers, found little change in this adjusted distribution between 1950 and 1970.[4] For example, according to their study, those households in the lowest 20 percent of the income distribution received 6.4 percent of the national net income in 1950 and 6.7 percent in 1970; at the other end of the distribution, the percentage of the net national income going to those households in the top 20 percent declined from 39.9 percent in 1950 to 39.1 percent in 1970.[5] Based on more recent studies of

[4]See Morgan Reynolds and Eugene Smolensky, *Public Expenditures, Taxes, and the Distribution of Income: The United States, 1950, 1961, 1970* (New York: Academic Press, 1977).

[5]Ibid. In correcting income distribution figures to account for tax payments and the value of transfers, economist Frank Levy found a little more shift toward equality than did Reynolds and Smolensky. See Frank Levy, *Dollars and Dreams: The Changing American Income Distribution* (New York: Russell Sage Foundation, 1987), pp. 196–97. Levy estimated that those in the lowest 20 percent of the income distribution received 5.8 percent of the nation's income in 1949 and 7.3 percent in 1984. He estimated that those in the highest 20 percent of the income distribution received 39.3 percent of the nation's income in 1949 and 36.8 percent in 1984. Levy's general conclusion was that "The [adjusted] income distribution became moderately more equal through the late 1960s and early 1970s but became less equal thereafter." Ibid. A more recent

the distribution of income, after adjusting for transfers and taxes, Robert Haveman concluded that "In spite of massive increases in federal government taxes and spending, we are about as unequal in 1988 as we were in 1950. . . . By 1988, those at the end of the income line had not moved closer to the middle, expensive efforts notwithstanding."[6]

It should be pointed out that studies showing little change in the adjusted distribution of income over time do not imply that government transfer programs have not reduced income inequality. There is still the counterfactual problem of knowing what the trend in the distribution of income would have been in the absence of the government transfer programs. There is evidence that the income distribution of different countries is very stable over time,[7] and so a basis exists for concluding that government transfers really have had little if any effect on the distribution of income in the United States. It has been argued, however, that changes have occurred in the economy and population that would have caused an increase in income inequality without government transfers. For example, after a long period over which average weekly earnings grew at 2 to 2.5 percent annually, this growth stopped in 1973, with almost no increase in average weekly earnings occurring from 1973 through 1985. Also, the percentage of the population that is young or old, and therefore more likely to have low incomes, has increased over the last few decades.[8] Of importance in this regard is the fact that there has been a large increase in the percentage of female-headed households in recent years. With these changes in mind, Haveman

study by the Bureau of the Census concluded, after adjusting incomes for taxes paid and benefits received, that those in the lowest 20 percent of the income distribution received 4.7 percent of U.S. income. See David Wessel, "Benefits Beat Taxes as Income Equalizer," *Wall Street Journal*, December 28, 1988. That suggests that the poorest receive a smaller percentage of the national income than the previously cited studies revealed. The Bureau of the Census study, however, did not provide an estimate of the income distribution for earlier years, so it does not, by itself, yield information on the trend in the income distribution.

[6]See Robert Haveman, *Starting Even: An Equal Opportunity Program to Combat the Nation's New Poverty* (New York: Simon and Schuster, 1988), p. 121.

[7]See Vincent J. Tarascio, "The Pareto Law of Income," *Social Science Quarterly* 54 (December 1973): 525–33.

[8]Although the elderly have lower than average incomes, they have significantly higher than average wealth. Bureau of the Census, *Statistical Abstract of the United States: 1988* (Washington: Government Printing Office, 1988), p. 440.

qualified his statement quoted above by adding, "While the efforts of the government were effective in offsetting the increase in inequality generated by the market, they did not override the forces associated with the 'new inequalities.'"[9]

The decline in average weekly earnings certainly reduces the income of the country, but there is no reason to believe that it has had any particular influence on the distribution of income. Also, although there are many factors that lie behind the sudden stop in the growth in earnings, there can be little doubt that the large increase in social welfare transfers that began in the mid-1960s was a contributing cause. As discussed earlier, these transfers necessarily reduce the incentive to engage in productive activities by both those who receive them and those who pay for them. And although there are no studies that reach definitive conclusions on the issue, there is evidence that part of the increase in female-headed households is explained by increased social welfare spending. In addition, there is evidence suggesting that this spending has increased the number of babies born out of wedlock, a group extremely vulnerable to poverty.[10] To the extent that trends exist that are causing greater inequality, they are partly the result of government programs designed to reduce inequality.[11]

Some Good News

Most discussions of poverty in America paint a dismal picture of the plight of the poor while arguing that government transfer programs have helped the poor by preventing their situation from being much worse than it is. The policy conclusions arising from these discussions are typically that government programs should be expanded because so much more remains to be done. It has recently been argued, however, that government has been more

---

[9]See Haveman, p. 121.

[10]See Morley D. Glicken, "Transgenerational Welfare Dependency," *Journal of Contemporary Studies* 4 (Summer 1981): 31–41.

[11]Haveman acknowledged that problem when he wrote:

Government efforts to bring people together were being undermined by countervailing forces—demographic changes, labor market changes, and economic changes—which made the benefits of government difficult to discern. *Indeed, in some ways the programs actually fostered the new inequalities.* Haveman, p. 120 (emphasis added).

effective at helping the poor—indeed, far more effective—than most people realize. And because government transfers have already done so much to shift the income distribution in favor of the poor, it is unrealistic to expect government to do any more to help the poor by shifting the income distribution further in their favor.[12]

Certainly there is compelling evidence that the figures on income distribution most commonly cited as evidence that poverty is a serious problem overstate the income inequality that actually exists. The most commonly used measure of income inequality in the United States comes from Bureau of the Census data on the distribution of money income. For 1990 the census data indicate that the families in the top 20 percent of the income distribution received 46.6 percent of all income while the families in the bottom 20 percent received only 3.9 percent. These figures suggest that the richest 20 percent are nearly 12 times better off financially than the poorest 20 percent. Fortunately, the poor are better off economically than these figures indicate.

A major problem with using census data to determine the degree of income inequality is that they do not include the value of in-kind transfers. That is a serious deficiency given that in-kind transfers account for 70 percent of the value of means-tested transfers. Also, the value of what the poor consume is a better measure of their economic well-being than their monetary income. And according to the Consumer Expenditure Survey of the Bureau of Labor Statistics, the poor spend far more on consumption than they receive in income. For example, according to the 1985 survey, consumer units in the bottom 20 percent of the income distribution spent on average $11,006 on consumption, which was three times as great as their before-tax income.[13] Much of this difference between consumption expenditure and income is explained by the fact that most of those whose income in a given year is low have sufficient wealth to

---

[12]That is roughly the position taken by Edgar K. Browning, "Inequality and Poverty" *Southern Economic Journal* 55 (April 1989): 819–30; Edgar K. Browning and William R. Johnson, "The Trade-Off between Equality and Efficiency," *Journal of Political Economy* (April 1984): 175–203; and Edgar K. Browning and William R. Johnson, "The Cost of Reducing Inequality," *Cato Journal* 6 (Spring/Summer 1986): 85–109.

[13]See Browning, p. 821.

maintain a reasonable standard of living. It is worth noting in this regard that the average net wealth of those families whose incomes in 1983 indicated that they were poor was $30,000.[14] That points to another serious deficiency with the census data on the income distribution. Because these data look at measured income over a single year, they overstate the degree of income inequality that exists over a longer time horizon. Even in the extreme case in which everyone would have exactly the same lifetime income, the pattern with which they receive that income over time would be such that income differences, probably large differences, would exist during any given year.[15]

The fact that income inequality is not as large as people are led to believe by commonly cited statistics does not imply that poverty is no problem. But the evidence showing that those in the bottom of the income distribution are consuming significantly more than their incomes (as measured by the Bureau of the Census) can support has to be considered good news by anyone who is genuinely concerned about the economic well-being of the poor. The news does not support the view, however, that the poor are better off economically than most people seem to realize because government transfers have reduced the inequality in the income distribution. It has always been true that, on average, those with low incomes in any given year consumed more than their current incomes. People whose incomes are low usually manage to avoid sharp drops in their consumption by using previously accumulated wealth, borrowing against future earnings, or receiving transfers from private or public sources. If, as seems to be the case, government programs have done little to change the distribution of income net of transfers and taxes, there is little reason to believe that government programs

[14]See Sawhill, p. 1079.

[15]By largely ignoring the problems associated with using census income data, a spate of recent books have concluded that during the last 20 or so years the distribution of income in the United States has become less equal, with the poor falling farther behind. See Robert B. Reich, *The Work of Nations* (New York: Alfred A. Knopf, 1991); Kevin Phillips, *The Politics of the Rich and Poor* (New York: Random House, 1990); Robert Kuttner, *The End of Laissez-Faire* (New York: Alfred A. Knopf, 1991); and Barry Bluestone and Bennett Harrison, *The Great U-Turn* (New York: Basic Books, 1988).

have noticeably affected the distribution of consumption by changing the borrowing and dissaving decisions that people make in response to variations in their incomes.

There is another piece of news that has to be considered as good news and that is taken as evidence that government transfers can and do help the poor. There can be no doubt that government transfer programs, primarily social security, have improved the economic situation of the elderly. The proportion of the elderly whose incomes are below the poverty level declined from 35.2 percent in the late 1950s to 12.4 percent in the late 1980s.[16] As desirable as the improved economic status of the elderly may be, their success at securing large transfers from government is completely consistent with our view of a competitive political process. One would expect that as decisions affecting income become more politicized, the elderly would improve their relative position in the income distribution. The elderly have more free time than most, which explains why they are more likely to vote and take part in organized interest groups than are the nonelderly. This fact, coupled with the fact that the elderly constitute a rapidly increasing percentage of the population, provides politicians with a strong incentive to respond to the demands placed on them by senior citizens.

The success of the elderly in the political competition for government transfers, however, has not necessarily done anything to reduce their overall income inequality. Although the elderly have lower incomes than the rest of the population, they also have far more wealth than average. And the social security system, which transfers so much income to the elderly, is not a means-tested program and it pays the highest benefits to those who earned the most during their working years and who are in no sense poor. So social security does less to reduce income equality even among the poor than might be thought.[17]

Furthermore, social security is financed by a regressive payroll tax that imposes a greater burden as a percentage of income on

[16]See Sawhill, p. 1084. The elderly are now less likely to have incomes below the poverty line than are the nonelderly.

[17]Although the money income distribution of the elderly has become somewhat more equal since 1967, it is still more unequal than the money income distribution for the entire population. See Haveman, p. 253, and Levy, p. 193.

those with lower incomes and that, it is estimated, will soon raise more revenue than the federal income tax.[18] Also, social security surely diverts funds away from other government programs that could do more to concentrate help on those who are genuinely disadvantaged. Therefore, although social security may appear to have reduced income inequality when the situation of the elderly is considered in isolation, it has probably done little to reduce inequality in the overall income distribution.

Hoping for a Bigger Piece of a Smaller Pie

Even if government transfer programs do increase the share of the national income going to the poor, it does not follow that the poor are benefiting from the programs. There can be no doubt that general economic growth and productivity are adversely affected by government transfers. Unless transfers increase the share of the national income going to the poor by a greater percentage than they reduce national income, they will reduce the absolute level of income that the poor receive. Those who put their faith in government transfers to reduce poverty have to hope that somehow political competition will increase the slice of the economic pie going to the poor by an amount sufficient to offset the resulting decrease in the size of the overall pie. The evidence we have presented on the equalizing effect of government transfers on the distribution of income does not offer much support for this hope. But even if the aggregate effect of government transfers were to significantly shift national income into the bottom part of the income distribution, there would still be compelling reasons for believing that over the long run the poor would be made poorer by government transfer activity.

Typically, the studies that attempt to determine the adverse effect of taxes and transfers on labor supply and investment decisions are measuring only *short-run* effects. But studies have shown that it can take decades before adjustments to the disincentives imposed by taxes and transfers are complete.[19] Reducing the incentive to engage in productive employment will have less effect on the decisions of those who have already prepared themselves for a career

[18]See Haveman, p. 116.

[19]See Charles Stuart, "Swedish Tax Rates, Labor Supply, and Tax Revenues," *Journal of Political Economy* 89 (October 1981): 1020–38.

and are currently in the workforce than it will on the decisions of those who have yet to enter the workforce. Investment in both physical and human capital sometimes take years to complete and become fully productive, and so the negative productivity effects of reducing current investment will manifest themselves fully only with a long delay. These response lags imply that the effectiveness of transfers to increase the income of the poor will erode over time, and that the negative impact of transfers on economic productivity will increase over time. The longer that transfer programs are available, the more some people will substitute publicly provided income for privately earned income, and therefore the transfers will do less to increase the income of the recipients. And the longer that economic decisions are distorted by the transfers and the taxes necessary to finance them, the greater will be the gap between what national income could have been and what it actually is.

To illustrate the gap, it is useful to consider a simple hypothetical example of two economies, economy A and economy B, that both begin with a $1 trillion net national income. It is assumed that the government of economy A actively transfers income from one group to another through a host of social welfare, farm, and trade-restriction programs. The government of economy B is assumed to confine its activities to establishing a setting that facilitates productive market interaction, and it makes no effort to alter the distribution of income that emerges from the market. It is further assumed that as a result of the two governments' differences in transfer activity, economy A grows at the rate of 3 percent per year and economy B grows at the rate of 4 percent per year.[20]

After 25 years, economy A will have a net national income of $2.09 trillion and economy B will have a net national income of $2.67 trillion. In other words, economy B will be 27.75 percent wealthier than economy A. If the overriding objective is to increase

[20]It should be pointed out that that represents a 33 percent difference in the growth rate between the two economies, using the growth rate of economy A as the base. That is a nontrivial difference, and some will see it as assuming an unrealistically high cost associated with transfer payments. The unrealistic assumption in our view is that of a government that confines itself within the limits required for maximum economic productivity, not the assumed difference in growth rates between an economy with an active transfer policy and an economy without one. Therefore, although we do not believe a government limited to the extent assumed here is a likely possibility, we do believe that our example provides a reasonable assessment of the benefits of such a government.

the income of the poor, then the government of economy A will have to alter its income distribution by enough to add over 27 percent to the income going to the poor to achieve that objective. We believe that the evidence on the ability of government to alter the income distribution indicates that no democratic government is likely to be able to permanently increase the share of the national income going to the poor by such a high percentage. And even if a government could increase the share going to the poor by 27 percent, the poor in our example would still be absolutely no better off after 25 years. The nonpoor are absolutely worse off from the very beginning, of course. And the situation gets exponentially worse for everyone as more time passes.

There is yet an additional problem with helping the poor with government transfers. Assume that government transfer policy can increase the income of those under the official poverty line by enough to offset the loss they suffer from the decline in general productivity and that it can do so permanently. As improbably successful as such a policy would be, it could still leave the poor worse off than a policy of no transfers. It is known that most people classified as poor do not remain poor for long (see chapter 8). Over half of those who are considered poor will move out of poverty within three years.[21] Although almost 25 percent of the population was considered poor during at least one year between 1969 and 1978, only one person in 20 was considered poor for five or more years during that ten-year period.[22] That means that even if transfers at every point increase the income of those who are considered poor but reduce the income of those who are not considered poor, those who receive benefits while poor may still be worse off because of their higher taxes and lower incomes when not poor.

It is useful for illustrative purposes to make two further assumptions. First, those who are poor at any one time will on average be classified as poor only 50 percent of the time in the future. Second, the net effect of all transfer programs is to increase the incomes of those who are poor by 20 percent and lower the incomes of those who are not poor by 20 percent. Under these assumptions, people

[21]Greg Duncan, *Years of Poverty, Years of Plenty* (Ann Arbor: University of Michigan Press, 1984).

[22]See Greg J. Duncan and Saul D. Hoffman, "Welfare Dynamics and the Nature of Need," *Cato Journal* 6 (Spring/Summer 1986): 31–54.

could expect their incomes to be lower over the long run because of the transfers. Because a 20 percent increase in an income that is below the poverty line is less than a 20 percent decrease in an income that is above the poverty line, even the poor (that is, those who expect to be poor 50 percent of the time) will have their expected incomes lowered by the transfer program. We make no claim for the realism of this example. It overstates the average amount of time that the current poor will remain poor, is overly generous in the assumed effectiveness of government's ability to alter the income distribution in favor of the poor, and ignores the negative effect that transfers have on economic growth. The purpose is to show that even a transfer program that is apparently effective at transferring income to the poor may reduce their long-term well-being.[23]

When most people think of government transfer programs, they automatically assume that the programs, on balance at least, assist those who are poor. That suggests to us that most people too readily confuse the rhetoric of political action with the reality of political action. We have argued that a realistic view of the political process provides little reason for believing that government transfer programs have helped the poor, but ample reason for believing that they have harmed the poor, at least over the long run. At the very minimum, the analysis and evidence suggest that skepticism rather than trust is the proper response to those who recommend more government spending to alleviate the inequalities of the marketplace. Indeed, we believe that public skepticism toward government transfers, no matter how noble the stated objective, is a necessary step in making the most effective use of government to help the poor. But before continuing with the argument behind this view, we need to make sure that our readers understand not only what we are arguing up to this point, but what we are not arguing as well.

---

[23]It should be pointed out that the example does not explicitly account for the fact that a small percentage of the population will be poor all or most of the time. Of course, a program that is effective at transferring to the poor an amount of income that is more than sufficient to offset the loss they suffer from the resulting productivity decline will help the permanently poor. But even the permanently poor will be worse off with transfer programs that are more effective in reducing economic productivity than in altering the income distribution in the favor of the poor.

The Transfer Trap

It is easy to read into our rather pessimistic discussion certain conclusions and recommendations that are not there. We are not arguing, for example, that if government transfer programs were summarily eliminated, the problem of poverty would be eliminated. As we emphasize throughout this book, no matter how efficiently the marketplace is operating, people will suffer from economic failure. Because of the opportunities and general wealth generated in market economies, most poverty will be temporary and moderate. But it cannot be denied that some people will suffer deprivation if left to fend for themselves in the competition for market rewards. Many of them would be provided for through private charitable activity, but some would not. And it can be argued that private charity would be insufficient, given the needs of many of the desperately poor. Our point here is not that the problem of poverty can be adequately addressed by the market, but that it is addressed in an extremely costly and inadequate way by government. Despite government spending in excess of $100 billion a year on programs expressly designed to assist the poor (not to mention additional hundreds of billions of dollars on transfer programs that are often presented as necessary to prevent poverty), there remain large numbers of poor in the United States today. Indeed, the number of poor and the degree of their poverty are likely greater because of government transfer programs.

The explanation of government's general inability to help the poor by shifting income from the upper portion of the income distribution to the lower portion is not an argument that no government programs are helping the poor. Our discussion is completely consistent with the observation that some government programs, considered alone, do help the poor, even over the long run. The problem is that for every program that helps the poor, there are other programs that harm them. The solution to this problem may seem simple: keep the programs that are improving the long-run prospects of the poor and eliminate those that are not.[24] The problem with this solution, and the problem that lies at the heart of

[24]For example, Haveman argued that income inequality can be reduced with no sacrifice in economic efficiency if policymakers can "identify and implement those policies that simultaneously promote both efficiency and equality. Those that sacrifice both should be abandoned." Haveman, p. 44.

our discussion here, is that the programs that harm the poor are supported by interests that politically are just as strong as, if not stronger than, those interests that favor programs that help the poor. Through the process of legislative logrolling, support for effective programs is obtained only by providing reciprocal support for programs that harm the poor.[25] The result is a package of programs that cannot be unbundled easily for the purpose of discarding some and keeping others.

And even if those transfer programs that harm the long-run interests of the poor could be eliminated suddenly and surgically, it is not clear from our discussion that it would be wise to do so. Let us posit the case of a welfare program with incentives that have enticed recipients into behavior that has left them worse off than they would have been had the program never existed. Having adjusted to such a program, recipients would experience genuine suffering in the short run if the program were suddenly scaled back or eliminated. Welfare recipients cannot develop instantly the skills and earning potential they would have developed in the absence of the welfare program. From the perspective of individuals who have failed to develop productive skills, who have children they cannot support, and who have absorbed an attitude of dependency from their surroundings, the short run over which they would be harmed by the elimination of the welfare program could turn out to be a significant period of time. Ideally, such a program would be eliminated gradually, with those who are already dependent on it being weaned slowly, but with it being made increasingly difficult for the program to be extended to new recipients.

Given the prevailing public view that government has not only the obligation but also the ability to help the poor, there is little concern that government transfers to the poor will be suddenly eliminated or even reduced greatly. The short-run trauma to the dependent poor resulting from any huge reduction in welfare payments would result in vivid images of suffering reported in dramatic news accounts. The public response to the perceived suffering would provide "compassionate" politicians with an opportunity to

---

[25]Haveman was not unaware of this problem. See Haveman, p. 43. However, when presenting his proposed reform, he did not address the problem of motivating political decisionmakers to eliminate the programs he wanted eliminated and to implement those he wanted implemented.

point to the "callousness" of rival politicians. Tremendous political pressure to reverse the cuts in welfare payments would be brought to bear on those politicians responsible for the cuts.

Several implications emerge. The greater the failure of welfare programs, as measured by the degree to which recipients become dependent on them, the more politically entrenched the programs become. The greater the recipient dependency promoted by welfare programs, the greater the transitional costs associated with scaling back or eliminating them. The long-run benefits associated with the elimination of many welfare programs may be significant, but they will be heavily discounted, if not ignored altogether, by a myopic political process. Therefore, once the political process has traveled very far down the transfer path and recipient groups have had time to respond to the incentives generated by transfer programs, it is not easy to turn back even though the long-run benefits of doing so would greatly exceed the short-run costs. The political process is easily caught in a transfer trap from which there is no easy or obvious escape.

Although we have been emphasizing the transfers associated with welfare programs, our discussion also applies to the difficulty of reducing transfer programs in general. And any attempt to improve the long-term well-being of the poor by reducing transfers would be ineffectual and probably counterproductive if transfers to the poor were reduced while transfers to the nonpoor were not.

Is there any hope for reversing the expansion in government transfers in general? And even more problematic, is there any hope of doing so without also cutting back those few transfers that actually do improve the prospects of the poor? We are convinced that the interests of the poor would be best served by severely restraining the ability of government to reward special privileges and transfers to those who are best able to exert political pressure. We recognize, however, that any attempt to reduce government transfers will meet resistance from organized interests, each of which will be competing to protect its own political privileges. All of the evidence we present seems to suggest that the poor will come out on the losing end of such competition. For the very reason the poor have not been very successful at competing for an expanding set of transfers, we cannot expect them to be very successful at competing for a contracting set of transfers.

The best hope for helping the poor is by reducing the scope of negative-sum political competition and increasing the scope of positive-sum market competition. That hope cannot be realized, however, as long as government is seen as the best vehicle through which people can exercise their feelings of compassion. Compassion exercised through the political process is invariably subverted by powerful interest groups to protect themselves from the discipline and failures of the marketplace. The result is an undermining of the productive market process that offers the best hope for those who are the true objects of compassion. The poor would realize greater benefit from government if the prevailing public attitude were hostile toward government attempts to help those threatened by or suffering from economic failure.

Soft-Hearted Results from a Hard-Hearted Approach

Economist Alan Blinder wrote a much-discussed book in 1987 in which he argued for government policy that is soft-hearted in its objectives but hard-headed in its approach.[26] Few can disagree that such an approach to government policy would be desirable. Who can object to achieving compassionate objectives as efficiently as possible through a hard-headed policy approach? It would seem callous to argue against a soft-hearted and hard-headed approach to public policy. But there are reasons for believing that attempts to use government for soft-hearted purposes is incompatible not only with hard-headed (efficient) approaches but also with soft-hearted outcomes. Soft-hearted objectives, when sought through the political process, tend to generate soft-headed (inefficient) approaches that result in hard-hearted outcomes. The outcomes of the political process are more likely to be what most people identify as compassionate when the approach of the political process is what most people see as callous.

If public sentiment is favorably disposed toward the use of government power to pursue compassionate objectives, there will be no shortage of such objectives that are put forth and that will receive public support. The necessary result of this political compassion is that an increased share of the nation's income will be subject to the control of political discretion.

[26]Alan S. Blinder, *Hard Heads, Soft Hearts: Tough-Minded Economics for a Just Society* (New York: Addison-Wesley, 1987).

149

It is theoretically possible, of course, that this expanded political discretion could be used to advance efficiently the noble objectives favored by the general public. However, although the general public may determine the broad direction of government policy, it will be organized interests, in competition with each other, that will determine the actual outcomes of government policy within the broad limits established by public sentiment.

In the case of the genuinely compassionate objective of reducing poverty, the excessive cost of government action can offset completely any good that is realized by the limited progress that is made. General economic inefficiency that has resulted from government transfers has likely more than offset any reduction in the inequality of the income distribution that has resulted. No matter how compassionate the objective of poverty reduction, little claim on people's sense of compassion can be made by policies that make the poor worse off absolutely.

The more general point here, however, is that as long as there exists widespread sympathy for using government power to solve a wide range of social problems, two unfortunate and related consequences will follow. First, discretionary government power will be created that will be abused by organized interest groups. Second, government will attempt to do a host of things that it is either incapable of doing or capable of doing only poorly and at costs that exceed the benefits.

That suggests that a necessary condition for controlling the harm done by special-interest political influence is a widespread distrust, even hostility, toward discretionary government power, not unlike that which existed at the time the U.S. Constitution was drafted and debated and which continued to characterize public opinion for the first 150 years of U.S. history. Only a pronounced public skepticism toward government can overcome the tendency for people to feel good about supporting government programs that purport to do good with power that will be controlled by narrowly motivated interests. Little good would be sacrificed, and much mischief would be avoided, if the voting public were skeptical of any government proposal to confiscate the wealth of one group for the express purpose of transferring it to another. That requires a public that is hard-hearted in that it rejects the soft-hearted sentiments that are always used to justify government transfers.

150

Such a hard-hearted public attitude toward government (we would call it an attitude of healthy skepticism) would accomplish one thing that we are confident would serve the interests of the poor as well as the nonpoor. It would prevent the further expansion of government transfer programs. There is no doubt that some individuals will continue to argue that any constraint on government transfers will hurt the poor. But that is simply not true, especially over the long run. To recommend limiting government transfers is not to lack compassion and concern for the poor. Quite the contrary. Does anyone really believe that if government doubled the percentage of the national income devoted to transfer programs, the distribution of income would be changed in favor of the poor? The far more likely result would be a reduction in economic growth that would leave the poor with less income—and less opportunity to move up the economic ladder through their own productive efforts.

Ideally, public skepticism toward government transfers would go beyond stopping the growth in transfer programs, and, over time, it would generate the political pressure needed to actually start reducing the size of the transfers. And there are reasons to believe that the poor would benefit more from such a reduction in government transfers than they would from simply halting the growth of transfers. A public that is aware of its inability to control the influence that special interests exert over transfer programs once those programs have received public approval is more likely to penetrate through the rhetoric of noble purpose that surrounds all transfer programs. Such a public will be less likely to give its approval to programs that transfer vast amounts of wealth from those with average and below average incomes to those with above average incomes. It would be those transfer programs that are targeted primarily to those who have a legitimate claim on the public's sympathy that will be in the best position to maintain public funding.

It would remain the case that organized interests would be able to control the details of such programs, which consequently would be less effective at helping the poor than they could be. But transfer programs aimed primarily at the poor obviously do more to benefit the poor than do transfer programs aimed at the nonpoor. Even if the absolute level of transfers to the poor went down as a result of increased public skepticism toward all transfer programs, the poor would likely still benefit from a relative increase in the amount of transfers received, with government's effect on the income distribution more likely to favor the poor. And furthermore, with a reduction in government transfers and the perverse incentives they create, there would be a larger national income and therefore more income for the poor even if their income share did not increase.

Concluding Comments

Attempts to be soft-hearted through the political process are exploited by organized special interests and result in soft-headed public policy. The best hope for the type of hard-headed policy required if the prospects of the poor are to be improved is a public attitude that is profoundly skeptical of benefits that can be realized from discretionary political power.

10. The Virtue of Economic Failure and the Failure of Political Virtue

When making a case for any program, project, or system, the temptation is strong to disassociate that which is favored from any responsibility for failure. Failures that cannot be denied are claimed to be isolated incidents that should not be considered inherent features of that for which the case is being made. The argument is that—with the proper adjustment, fine tuning, and commitment— the failures can be eliminated and only success will remain. Although such an approach in making a case for a market economy is tempting, and is often attempted, our message in this book is that the case for a market economy has to not only accept but also embrace the failures that are the result of market competition. The most honest and ultimately most compelling case for the market system depends upon the recognition that failures are an inherent and constant feature of the market process. The overall success of market economies depends critically on the information and motivation that can be created only by economic failures. Any attempt to consider economic failures as isolated incidents in the capitalist system ignores an essential ingredient in the economic success of that system.

The purpose of this book is to defend the market economy against its critics by emphasizing the economic failures of the market economy and the virtue of those failures. The most effective case against a market system has always been that although market competition may produce great wealth, it does so without regard for how that wealth is distributed or who is left behind. The marketplace is seen as littered with the victims of economic failures that take the form of bankruptcy, unemployment, and pockets of poverty. The inevitable conclusion is that government action is needed in the form of programs, transfers, and restrictions on market competition to moderate the unfairness and the failures in the marketplace. Unfortunately, as long as this argument is accepted, there is always a justification, in the name of virtue, for expanding the economic role of government, regardless of how large that role becomes.

Substituting government control for market competition cannot eliminate competition or the failure that results from competition. Expanding the economic role of government substitutes political competition for market competition, with the resulting failures doing far less to promote productivity than do the failures in the competitive marketplace. The failures that result from political competition are diffused and disguised, and they provide none of the information or motivation necessary for the creation of wealth. Expanding government does nothing to reduce economic failure, but does much to reduce economic success, and thus generates additional economic problems that can be and constantly are blamed on the market and used to justify yet more government.

Accordingly, the case for the market requires more than just an understanding of the productive role of failure in the market economy. Although economic failure brings about productive responses in the marketplace, it also can and commonly does bring about destructive responses in the political arena. No matter how efficiently economic failure directs efforts and resources into their most valuable uses, those individuals who suffer from such failure cannot be expected to look beyond their personal distress and take comfort in the general economic benefits being generated. The private interest of each individual threatened with economic failure is best served by government protection against that failure. And the desire on the part of each individual and organized group for government protection is not moderated in the least by the fact that such protection increases overall economic failure, or that everyone is worse off, including those receiving protection, when that protection is generalized over much of the economy. Every group sees the advantage in lobbying for a government exemption to the discipline of market competition regardless of how successful other groups are at obtaining similar exemptions. The best possible situation is to obtain protection while everyone else is subject to the full force of marketplace competition, and the worst possible situation is to be denied protection in an economy rendered grossly inefficient by protection for everyone else.

In the absence of strict limits on the ability of politicians to accommodate the demands of organized interests, the strong tendency is for market competition, which is generally wealth producing, to be replaced with political competition, which is often wealth reducing. When individuals see government as the vehicle by which they can escape the economic failures of the marketplace, there is a headlong rush for a smorgasbord of political privileges that undermine the market discipline upon which the overall success of the economy depends. The resulting political competition is one in which everyone is an eventual loser, with the possible exception of a very few whose political power allows them to capture a sufficiently large slice of a diminishing economic pie. The dictators, and a few of their henchmen, in even the most impoverished countries may do better by draining their national wealth into Swiss bank accounts than they could by engaging in productive market activity. But for the overwhelming majority, political competition is a losing game. Political competition certainly is a losing proposition for the poor, who find that it is better for them to have a tiny percentage of a large economic pie than a tiny percentage of a small one.

Despite widespread opinion, the argument that market competition leaves a constant stream of failure in its wake does not constitute a valid case against the market. In the real world of scarcity, imperfect information, unpredictable changes, and the need to coordinate the action of millions of economic agents around the globe, failure is a ubiquitous feature of all economies, no matter what form they take. The case for the market is not that it eliminates failures, but that it uses the failures that are scattered throughout the economy to generate the information and incentives necessary to produce an overall pattern of economic success. The biggest threat to the success of the market economy is not the self-correcting failures imposed by market competition, but the self-perpetuating failures imposed by political competition for government protection against the discipline of the marketplace.

Index

Political action
effect of, xii, 12
to improve public policy, 120–21
motivation for, 102
Political competition
outcomes of, 131–32
participation of the elderly in, 141
when substituted for market
competition, 154–55
Political failure, 12–13
Political institutions
development in former Soviet Union
of, 60
purpose of, 90
Political process
alteration of market outcomes,
78–79, 82–83
lack of accountability in, 102
as means to acquire influence, 98–99
perceived fairness of, xi–xii
response to economic failure, x,
11–12, 65
role of individual voter in, 94–98
in transfer of wealth to poor, 117–31
Politics
lack of responsibility in, 94
mobilizing support, 108, 123, 124
Poor, the
changing behavior of, 107
competition from the nonpoor,
130–31
in competitive process, 136
effect of political competition on,
117–31, 155
government help to, 105–9
hours of work without transfers, 110
as interest group, 122
public skepticism to help, 145
reducing incentives of, 109–10
spending on consumption of, 139–40
their response to help, 109–14
transfer programs for, 117, 142
well-being under welfare and
transfer programs, 134–36
See also Nonpoor, the
Poverty
cycle of, 9
effect of welfare on reducing, 134–35
inadequate government policy for,
xiii, 107, 146–49
incentives to avoid, 109–11, 131
moving in and out of, 12, 144–45,
146
persistence of, 106, 146
programs encouraging, 110–12
as result of economic failure, 9
under socialism, ix

Poverty gap, 125
Poverty professionals, interests of,
121–23
Poverty programs
cost to monitor effectiveness, 120
effect of, 110–11
interest groups contributing to,
121–22
proposed effective government, 106
rationale for many, 107
Price controls, 55–57
Prices
to communicate preferences, 79–80
determinants of market economy,
67–68
in former Soviet Union, 57
and private property, 47–49, 79–80
Private charities
conditions for contribution to, 116
effect of increased government
transfers on, 116
with government transfer programs,
108
role in reducing dependency, 112–14
Property rights
accountability under, 48–49
conditions for infringement on, 86
with enlarged government role, 99
protection and transfer of, 79
rule of, 46–47
See also Rules
Protectionism, 21–26, 129–30
Public assistance programs, 123–26
See also Poverty programs
Public employees, 1–2
See also Poverty professionals
Public goods
choice in financing of, 87
productive social order as, 86
Public interest
potential for interest groups to
dominate, 90–94
special interests proposals as, 93–94
Public opinion
effect of a constitution on, 101
required skepticism, 103, 145,
150–52
in response to failure, 1, 10, 102
Public policy
effect of compassionate, 103, 149–52
political action to improve, 120–21
to protect jobs, 25
in response to failure, 2, 10, 21,
25–26
See also Interest groups; Legislation;
Protectionism; Trade, international

Wealth
conditions for reduction of, 102
dependence on individual pursuits,
77–78
of the elderly, 141
under free-market capitalism, 51
function of failures in production of,
x–xi
of the poor, 117
transfer from non-politically to
politically organized of, 129–31
when government distributes or
transfers, 99–100, 133
Welfare programs
effectiveness of, 134–38

effect of, 111–13
effect on poor with and without,
134–49
increased funding for, 124
interest of poor in, 122–23
payments under, 110
See also Poverty programs; Public
assistance programs; Transfer
programs
Wessel, David, 136–37n5
Wilson, William Julius, 9n14

Yeltsin, Boris, 63

Zero-sum games, 72

About the Authors

Dwight R. Lee is Bernard B. and Eugenia A. Ramsey Professor of Private Enterprise and Economics at the University of Georgia, Athens. Richard B. McKenzie is Walter B. Gerken Professor of Enterprise and Society in the Graduate School of Management at the University of California, Irvine.

Both Lee and McKenzie are adjunct fellows at the Center for the Study of American Business at Washington University. They have collaborated on two previous books: *Regulating Government: A Preface to Constitutional Economics* (Lexington, Mass.: Lexington Books, 1987) and *Quicksilver Capital: How the Rapid Movement of Wealth Has Changed the World* (New York: Free Press, 1991). Both authors have written a number of other books and numerous articles for scholarly journals. They also have published commentaries in some of the country's major national newspapers, including the *Wall Street Journal, New York Times, Washington Post,* and *Christian Science Monitor.*